The Best of Joe Weider's
MUSCLE
& FITNESS
More
Training Tips
and Routines

The Best of Joe Weider's

MUSCLE & FITNESS

More Training Tips and Routines

Contemporary Books, Inc.
Chicago

Library of Congress Cataloging in Publication Data

Main entry under title:

More training tips and routines.

1. Bodybuilding—Addresses, essays, lectures.
1. Weider, Joe. II. Muscle & fitness.
GV546.5.M66 1982 646.7′5 82-45422
ISBN 0-8092-5594-4
ISBN 0-8092-5618-5 (pbk.)

All photos courtesy of the International Federation of Bodybuilders.

Published by Contemporary Books, Inc.
180 North Michigan Avenue, Chicago, Illinois 60601
Manufactured in the United States of America
Library of Congress Catalog Card Number: 82-45422
International Standard Book Number: 0-8092-5594-4 (cloth)
0-8092-5618-5 (paper)

Published simultaneously in Canada by
Beaverbooks, Ltd.
150 Lesmill Road
Don Mills, Ontario M3B 2T5
Canada

Contents

The Best of Joe Weider's

MUSCLE & FITNESS

More Training Tips and Routines

Secrets of Bodybuilding Longevity

by Frank Zane

Twelve weeks, ideally, is the amount of time I allow myself to get in contest shape. Over that period of time I continue using heavier and heavier weights, taking less rest between sets. I have always used the progressive resistance system, increasing the weight on each of three successive sets per exercise. I also progressively work up to five sets on some exercises over the 12-week period.

It takes 12 weeks for me to peak. I have to look that far ahead. I know from past experience that if I try to cram my buildup into a shorter period, I get hurt. I also have to plan my training cycles around my other interests, such as Zane Haven (where I teach bodybuilding) and book promotion tours. All of these activities take time and energy.

I took a month off from training this past year, and I felt the better for it. I lost a little body weight, but when I started training again, it shot back up. At this writing I have begun a new 12-week training program to be in peak condition for an upcoming book promotion tour.

The core of my approach is cycle training with gradually increasing intensity. In my workouts, I maintain a steady pace to avoid injury. I usually reach three strategically planned peaks during the year, two lesser ones, and a maximum one. I must cycle my training so that my other activities can be worked into the schedule. I think that's the key to longevity in bodybuilding.

You can be a flash in the pan, training all out, entering every contest, but you soon wear out. I've seen this happen to several good bodybuilders, and they've been forced to take layoffs for months, even years. Using a system like mine, you can be around forever—barring unforeseen circumstances. You also get better gradually as you learn more about yourself. And as you get older, you become more disciplined. Your lifestyle improves, making the bodybuilding effort itself easier.

When I started bodybuilding, it was a hobby, and I had to teach school to support myself. Now that I am a bodybuilding professional, I am using my former profession to teach bodybuilding. It's worked out very well for me.

The guy who comes to California and struggles to make ends meet will not get very far. Anxiety causes his bodybuilding to suffer. The older, more experienced bodybuilders have the advantage of maturity, discipline, and more stable living conditions. Up to a certain point you can make rapid improvement in this sport, but you have to learn to accept and use the smaller gains that come with maturity.

I think 12 weeks is the shortest training period you should allow yourself to achieve peak condition. This assumes that you have established a baseline condition during the off-season. You can't let yourself get far out of shape, and you shouldn't take a layoff unless you are in top shape. The layoff then gives you a fresh perspective and gets rid of any aches and pains. You approach a fresh training start as a beginner, doing only basic movements and limiting the amount of work. If you have taken a month's layoff, the muscles respond rapidly to training.

During your layoff, don't avoid the gym completely. Instead, work two weak body parts, five sets each, a total of 10 sets per workout. This gives your weak points a head start when you commence serious training again. All the body parts will then progress more proportionately because the weak points have been stimulated while the others have remained dormant. This procedure tends to change the look of your physique. I use this method regularly in my continual effort to change and improve my physique.

Bodybuilders who compete frequently always seem to look the same. The ones who look different are those who compete once a year, or once every two years. But if you wait too long before competing, you might experience diminishing returns. I think a two-year wait is the maximum.

I seek change in my physique because I think that's the only way you can win these days. If you change enough, you have to win. There are no guarantees, of course, but every competitor likes to think that if he gets into the best shape of his life, he has a decent chance to win.

You can train properly only if you allow yourself enough time. In my life, I don't make sudden decisions to train. I have to phase into it. Actually, it takes more than *three* months to get into really good shape. It takes six months: you need three months to get in shape for the three months of final training.

I plan my training a year in advance. I can better coordinate my other activities with my training to reach the target date in peak condition.

The more I train, the stronger I get. As I continue handling heavier weights, my muscles get thicker. This coming year, purely from a standpoint of personal curiosity, I'm going to strive for quality in the amount of muscle mass that I build. I know that 30 to 40 sets per workout—following my training cycle of three days on and one day off—will do it. I'll do 3–4 sets per exercise, 6–10 reps. I'll use the Weider split system of training, working three body parts a day and calves every day.

On this program, I continue to get stronger, make more gains, and use heavier weights. In order to avoid injury from using heavy weights, or not to aggravate prior injuries, it is safest to do each exercise in near-perfect form. You don't get injured when the weight follows a groove.

The movements that tend to injure me are the ones in which I have to fight against a fixed position. For example, if I do Machine Presses after doing only Dumbbell Presses for a long period of time, I tend to get injured, especially if I go too heavy too fast. You can't budge from a locked-in position, can't move your shoulders or hands, so your spine takes the stress. When you can coordinate your movements in an exercise (such as Dumbbell Presses), you stand less chance of injury. I use barbell, dumbbell, cable, and machine exercises, but I have developed precise grooves in all of them.

The better your form in an exercise, the better muscle shape you'll get. You have more control over how the muscle develops when you purposely do the movements correctly. Ideally, you should develop an exact groove in each exercise, and exact timing—how fast you raise the weight, how slow you lower it, and how much rest you take between sets.

I use 6–10 reps in my upper-body exercises and 12–25 reps when training the legs. I only do one weighted abdominal exercise: Knee-Ins with the pulley around my feet. I would never do weighted Sit-Ups because they hurt the back. I am not interested in building the waist. I want to keep it small but defined, with deep, chiseled abdominals, obliques, serratus, and intercostals.

Teaching bodybuilding at Zane Haven has increased my motivation to train. I spent 13 years as a schoolteacher and I have always liked the idea of teaching. I believe a person should be an example of what he or she teaches. So instructing people at Zane Haven helps my own bodybuilding. It makes me conscientious and reinforces me. When I teach about vitamins, I make sure I take them every day.

You need this consistency as you get older. Time becomes precious. You can't wander from the path like you did when you were young, knowing that you had plenty of time to return. The need for motivation never lessens. In fact, it's motivation that makes my training sessions so effective.

Mental Nutrition: Feeding Your Mind with Powerful, Positive Thoughts

by Mike Shadick

If you're just starting out in bodybuilding, you might think that attaining your weight-training goals is largely a matter of lifting the right weights in the right way for the right number of repetitions. Important as all of this is, there is one factor that can and will play an even more important role in the attainment of your weight-training goals.

What is this all-important factor? The late Dr. Norman Vincent Peale, who may have known little about weight training per se but was one of the world's leading experts on the power of positive thinking, stressed that one's mental attitude is the single most important determining factor in the success of any human activity. For without the proper mental attitude, said Dr. Peale, whatever you endeavor to do is doomed to failure, or (at the very least) to a much, much lower level of success than you would attain with a proper mental attitude.

Exactly how does Dr. Peale's power of positive thinking apply to weight training? And, more specifically, what is the "right" mental attitude for a weight-training person that will guarantee him or her the highest level of success?

Many bodybuilders—beginners and professionals alike—approach weight training with an attitude which might be summed up in this manner: "Well, here comes another workout." Or, "I'm really gonna push myself today." Or even, "I'm sort of tired, but I've got to do this if I'm going to reach my goal."

You've probably said those things, or something pretty similar, to yourself many times. Well, there's nothing radically wrong with the mental attitude exemplified by those statements. But there's nothing really right about them, either! For, in every case, they indicate that you think, "It's me versus the weights." Furthermore, they indicate that you think the weights might sometimes win!

Well, let me tell you that the weights need *never* win. There is only one winner in weight training, and that's *you*! And I'm not just speaking about some of the time. I mean every single time you work out! And do you know why you're always the winner? It's because *you are superior*!

Superior to what? Not just to the weights themselves (you are their master!), but even to what you were yesterday! For through weight training, you are making yourself superior to

Rod Koontz built his award-winning body muscle by muscle, with iron, sound nutrition, and unrelenting positive thinking.

anything you've ever been before. That is not just a supposition; it's a fact.

I want you to do something. Sometime in the next day or two go to the place where you do your weight training. But this time, instead of working out with the weights, I want you just to look at them. While you are looking at them, I want you to say to yourself: *"I AM SUPERIOR!"*

This may come as a surprise to you, but the fact is that you're not only superior right now, you always have been! And if you tell yourself of your own superiority often enough, you will come to perceive how very true it is.

Note that this technique is the very opposite of brainwashing. It is, in effect, brain *clearing*! For you are wiping away the negative mental attitudes from your thinking, and replacing them with positive ones.

But alas, negative mental attitudes are every bit as powerful as positive ones. So just a word of warning. You can never relax your grip on a positive mental attitude. If you should ever stop thinking, "I'm superior," you will sink right back into your old (negative) ways of thinking.

In other words, a positive mental attitude is not something you can "acquire" and, once having acquired it, forget about. No, you must constantly feed it, so to speak. Fortunately, there are many ways in which a bodybuilder can maintain a positive mental attitude. Indeed, one of the most effective ways is to approach your entire weight-training program—today, tomorrow, and every day—in a truly superior, positive spirit. For you are superior!

Just how superior are you? *You're as superior as your attitude*. That is, if your attitude is inferior (i.e., negative), your weight-training results will be inferior also. But if your attitude is positive, then you will most assuredly attain your weight-training goals—whatever they may be!

How I Won the 1981 Mr. Olympia

by Dr. Franco Columbu

The following article is excerpted directly from Franco Columbu's personal diary, his notes on what he did and how he trained to win the 1981 Mr. Olympia title. We liked the directness and honesty of the style and decided simply to let Franco's own words speak for themselves.

Injured knee in 1976 "Strongest Man" competition right after the Olympia. Knee completely torn apart. Every time I tried to train, I hurt it again. Finally, found ways of training thighs with corrective exercises, but no Squats, Deadlifts, or anything heavy like that. Lots of Half-Leg Extensions, stretching, and walking up steps sideways to develop the sides of the knee.

After a few years I began doing light Squats. Took years. Tried to get in shape for the Olympia last year, but the knee was still too weak.

In February 1981, I went to Spain to do *Conan* movie and got way out of shape because I couldn't train. Jumped down from a rock and hurt the knee again. Thought it might be all over, that I wouldn't be able to train for the Olympia. Afraid I wouldn't be able to compete at all.

Got so depressed and out of shape, I didn't know how to start again. Decided simply to do stretching exercises. Then, in April, Gregory Harrison, the actor, asked if I would train him for TV movie, *For Ladies Only,* all about male strippers. I said, "Sure, for a good fee." I ended up training him and getting back into training myself. I was encouraged by this to get back into shape.

Did one hour training, one hour stretching, and one hour gymnastics, slowly building up the strength of the knee. In May, I decided that in June I would train nothing but arms (not my best point), thighs, and calves. Since my chest, back, and shoulders grow with little training, I would leave them alone. If, after that month, my arms looked better than ever and my thighs looked good, I would begin to train seriously for the Olympia.

All during June I worked out at World Gym and everyone asked, "What kind of training is this? One day, arms; next day, thighs and calves; next day, arms; and so on." They said, "What the hell is this? What about chest, back, abs, and shoulders?" I said, "Forget it. I know I can get them up any time. That doesn't worry me."

At the end of June I told myself that on the first day of July I would look at myself in the mirror, look at the other guys in World Gym, and decide if I should compete. There was Samir, Tom Platz, Chris Dickerson—even if they

never took their clothes off—and I liked the way I compared. So I said, "I'm going to train the month of July. Still a lot of arms and thighs and a little bit of chest, back, and shoulders. Arms three times a week; thighs and calves three times a week; chest, back, and shoulders once a week."

On August first I looked in the mirror and said, "Let's see if I look like the other guys." I looked in proportion. My weak points were up, and the other bodybuilders looked like always, like in every Grand Prix. Their weak points were still weak, their strong points still strong. Most of them were smooth—I'm never fat. I don't believe in bulking up a lot and then trying to get down the last month before the contest. I gain weight right up to the day of the contest.

In August, I started training without my shirt on and telling everybody that I was going to compete in the Olympia. Everybody said, "Oh, it's too late for you . . . only two months and 10 days." Every other contender told me he was going to win, and I said, "Sure." But I knew even in August that I was going to win. Because the other bodybuilders were putting so much energy into politics, and trying to get on the covers of magazines and get their articles published in *Muscle & Fitness.* They thought they could win by gaining popularity, by publicity in the magazines, and through calling organizers, officials, and anyone who might be judging.

I thought, "Let them do that. I'll put all of my energy into training. Then, at the last minute, when we get to the contest, all my energy will be in my body while theirs is out somewhere else."

My training in August consisted of 20 sets, back; 20 sets, chest; 15 sets, shoulders; 15 sets, triceps; 10–12 sets, biceps; 15 sets, thighs; and 10 sets, calves. The reason for this proportion: all the other bodybuilders were doing equal sets for every body part, so their good body parts kept getting better and their bad body parts stayed bad; their small muscles stayed small and overtrained, and their big muscles were undertrained.

So I gave the big muscles like chest and back a lot of sets and I did fewer sets for the smaller muscles like biceps, which can't handle more than 10 or 12 sets or they will burn out. This method gave me gains every day; I gained one or two pounds of muscle every week and lost fat at the same time. The other guys were gaining three or four pounds, including a lot of fat.

I was doing a lot of strange exercises. For example, Incline Curls to get the outside of the biceps. I wanted biceps on top of my biceps—because everybody knows that my chest, shoulders, and back are the best, but thinks my arms are skinny. I didn't want anyone to be able to say that. I wanted to develop three-head biceps, if possible! I wanted my thighs to look as good as anyone's, and my calves to look better. Look at the pictures and see the splits in my biceps. I got those only in the last months of training.

I started training every day with my shirt off. The others—Callender, Platz, Dickerson, Samir—were all covered up from head to toe. And not even taking showers when I was around. I found that a little bit disappointing. I would have liked to see what they looked like.

Arnold (Schwarzenegger): the type of person that loves excitement. Doesn't just go into the gym to get in shape; wants to get in shape and make a lot of noise, scream, and have fun. Bodybuilders get worried, too involved with their own thinking, but Arnold loves noise. So when I came in without my shirt on Arnold would tell everyone, "Franco's coming up all pumped up from downstairs." He'd say I pumped up and put oil on, even though I never did. He told some bodybuilders, "Franco just came in. You go downstairs and I bet you any money he is doing push-ups." He actually made people believe it, and they came downstairs looking, which I thought was the funniest thing.

Chris Dickerson: one day I go downstairs at World Gym and I catch him turning on the faucet to take a shower. He ran. He took the towel, took the clothes, got into his car, and went home to take a shower. Since then, he only took a shower when I wasn't there, or didn't shower at the gym. Other guys also went home to take showers. Like they had all decided to keep Franco wondering by keeping their clothes on.

I remember one day I came in and I heard Chris telling Roy Callender, "Roy, I only worry about you. I don't worry about Franco. Because, look: his shirt is off; he's all pumped up; he's out of proportion. You want to keep him wondering, don't take your clothes off." And Roy says, "I never take my clothes off." I overheard this and so did Eddie Giuliani, who told me Chris wasn't worried about me. So I say, "How big is his arm?" "Almost 17 inches," Eddie answers. "Go tell him my arm is 19 and looks better," I reply.

As time went on, I could see who was really training hard. I was, and so were Roy Callender and Tom Platz. In my opinion, we were the three people who were really training hard and would be at the top. Chris Dickerson trained pretty hard, but I was surprised he got it together because he was training with such light weights.

By September first I was already in better shape than all of them. Samir came to me and said, "I'm going to start cutting down." I said to him, "You had better cut down before the contest, not after it."

I actually overtrained every week. The overtraining broke down my fat. In the second week of September, I was supposed to go away, so I decided not to train for four days; I needed the rest. For four weeks I had not missed a training day, even Saturdays and Sundays. Besides, I was taking care of my chiropractic practice at the same time.

Schedule

7 am–9 am in the gym
9 am–6 pm adjusting patients
7 pm–9 pm back in the gym

On this Weider Double-Split schedule, I got my fat down to nothing. When I didn't train those four days I felt so good and rested.

Stage three of my preparation—from the tenth of September, only four weeks to go. Now gaining more slowly, only a pound a week. Trying to get my body weight up to 188. Figuring I would lose two or three pounds the last few days with the aggravation and being nervous and worried, and would get down to 185 or 186. But I wanted that body weight to be all muscle, no fat.

I trained nonstop until three days before the contest. I also went 2–3 times a week to an aerobics class at the Sports Connection. I wouldn't have done it except for Arnold. He told me, "Franco, I'm not going to help you in Ohio. I'm working there and I don't want to help you at all. Don't ask me who the judges are. You're my friend, but I don't want to talk to you about competing or about judges or anything. But you can talk about training every day. You call me anytime and I will go to the gym with you. That's where I can help you. But I don't want to talk about the Olympia."

Then he said, "Get ready and let's go to the Sports Connection." So we get there and he sticks me in a stretching class, and this is after I have already trained two hours. Then he takes me for one hour into an aerobics class with all these advanced people. I was so embarrassed. I looked like a turtle there moving around. Arnold says, "You've got to do it." Then we went upstairs to ride the stationary bicycles, and we broke a bicycle trying to see how fast we could make it go. We got up to 90 miles an hour or something, and the thing broke. And Arnold says, "Okay, let's leave now."

Another thing he did was to call the gym every day and ask if I was training. If I wasn't there, he would call me and ask why. Eddie Giuliani and Joe Gold were like two spies for Arnold. They had written down what time I got there, what time I left. They had two or three other people to watch and make sure I was training enough.

Arnold would also come to the gym and once in a while give me little things to do to make the muscles come out in a different place. One day he came to me and said, "I want you to do Front Squats on the machine, 10 sets, 20 reps, nonstop, and then you go home." And I tried that and it really worked. It got the outside sweep immediately.

Then another day he comes in and says, "I want you to do a Bent-Over Reverse Curl." I said, "What? What is that?" I had never seen it anyplace. He showed me how to take hold of a bar the reverse way, bend forward at a 40-degree angle, and then do the exercise. I did that and the outside head of the biceps came out in three days—came out like a balloon.

He showed me something on the Leg Extension machine I had never seen before. He said bring it up and hold it locked out for three seconds, which really burns. Joe Weider told me the same thing. He once made me do Extensions where you come up slow, hold it, and then go down slow, which is really torture. I tried it with him once, and I was hoping that I would never see him again when I was doing thighs.

Joe Weider came in one day when I was posing. I hit a double biceps and held it for one minute. Then, when I was exhausted, he said, "Okay, now flex." "How long should I flex?" I asked. "Flex from now until the show," he told me. "Flex in your sleep—that's how you'll increase your definition and density."

And once in a while Arnold came in and trained with me. That was also stimulating. And with all of these things, as we got closer to the contest, I was more and more sure I was going to win. Because the others weren't changing much and were always talking about calling people like Joe Weider, Jim Lorimer, Ben Weider, and Arnold. I would have been embarrassed to call these people.

I was aware of some of the political feeling—that the contest was fixed, that I was supposed to be the winner. But I felt that the best way to deal with that was to come into the contest in such good shape that they couldn't deny I was the best.

And I was the best. All the top guys were in good shape, but lacked something. Some guys had a lot of size, some guys had a lot of definition, but nobody but me had both. I had better proportions, more size, and more definition. I would have put Roy Callender second with Tom Platz and Chris Dickerson tied for third. Roy and Tom trained so hard I couldn't believe it.

I left town for a while before the contest to get some sun. I wanted to see if I could win a contest without any paint on my body. Everybody else there was painted but me. I just had on a little bit of oil. My clothes never got dirty. I was happy about that.

I finally got Samir to take his shirt off. The Italian press came to take pictures of me and I said, "Samir, do you want to be in the Italian magazines?" He said yes, so I told him to take his shirt off.

When I saw the guys backstage in Columbus I knew I was going to win; they all looked the same as always. They were all in great shape, every one of them. Even Danny Padilla had great definition. But a lot of them made the mistake of pumping up too much at the beginning. I knew the Prejudging would be long. If you pumped up too much, you would burn yourself out. "Okay," I said, "I'm not going to pump up."

So I went out for the first round without pumping up. You look at the scores: I got 96, Chris Dickerson 96, Roy Callender 96 in the first round. Then in the second round, I pumped up 15% or 20%, and they're still pumping up full power. Now I looked a little bigger and the judges were really impressed. In the third round, I pumped up 80% and the others were burned out. That is where I killed them. They got 96s again and I got 99.

I had choreographed my routine and I had good music. I came out and did a 4.5-minute posing routine, while nobody else's was longer than about two minutes. It was a shock for everyone. All the judges were giving me 20s; they couldn't believe that a routine could be that long and that good. I got five 20s and another 99. Chris was good but got a 97.

I think I won for many reasons. Physically, I had size, definition, and good proportion. And my posing was really exciting. Chris Dickerson looked good and his definition surprised me. I thought Callender looked really good, but he was just a little smooth, his skin was a little thick—and that's why he got fourth. Tom Platz looked as good as he could, but I don't think he has his proportions 100% correct yet.

Roy Callender is a good poser with a tremendous physique, but it is a mistake to point at his thighs. If the thighs are good, the judges will see it. Danny Padilla, too, pointed to his calves. If the judges can't see the calves, they don't deserve to be judges.

When the finalists were onstage, I thought I had won, but I felt I had done better during the day than at night. At night, Oscar State kept us from doing things. The crowd didn't like that. When they announced Roy Callender as fourth, I was sure I won, because I was more worried about Roy Callender than I was about Chris Dickerson.

Backstage, after the contest, Arnold said to me in German, "It's a booing contest just like last year." Why booing? When Roy Callender was doing his posing routine the tape with his music broke. Roy is a nice man, and the audience was on his side. When he was announced fourth, that's when they started booing the most. Then, when they announced Platz third, they were still booing. And then Dickerson second—the audience wanted Roy Callender there. I think the audience wanted the contest to be between Roy Callender and me. I have a tape of the contest and it shows this very clearly.

Who started the booing? Out of 5,000 people, I know who the first person booing was. Rick Wayne. And I asked him, "Rick, you were the first person to boo me. What are you doing?" And he said, "I was thinking of Australia." It was really funny.

I was aware of the problems because of Australia in 1980, but I never considered not competing. I just wanted to be so good that nobody would think my winning was political. When people have a chance to look at the comparison pictures, they will agree that I deserved to be the winner.

The truth is, all the competitors at Columbus were in good shape and I was lucky that my instincts told me to go all out and not trust that people would be out of shape.

Cycling Your Training Poundages

by Tom Platz

At the 1981 Mr. Olympia contest in Columbus I was in the best shape of my career. My upper body—arms, shoulders, back, everything—was on a par with my legs. I have worked hard the past three years developing the proportion everyone thought I would never attain.

My legs have always created a sensation. I took the Mr. Universe title three years ago, I believe, on the strength of my leg development. Though adequate, my upper body paled by comparison. I was determined to change that.

Simply working the upper body harder wasn't the answer. I had tried that, but it didn't work. No, gainful training is more subtle than that.

It has been about four years since I packed up and moved to the West Coast to become a champion bodybuilder. During that time, with considerable guidance from Joe Weider, I explored many training possibilities and eventually developed a system that worked best for me.

INSTINCTIVE TRAINING PRINCIPLE

Joe has constantly stressed the need for training instinctively. You assume you're relying on your instinct to guide you, but more often than not tradition and conscious dogma interfere. Instinctive training, I have learned, is a creative process, an art. And it's a difficult one because you're probing beneath your conscious mind into an area full of darkened passageways that can lead to treasured training discoveries.

MUSCLE GROWTH

One thing I have learned is that "shocking" the muscle—not once, but constantly—is necessary to stimulate growth and increase strength. Given a task, muscle tends to disregard further direction and lapses into habit. A bodybuilder has many available techniques to produce the necessary muscle stimulation. For example, he can use slow, continuous movements or heavy semi-cheat movements. Each of these techniques creates a new cycle of growth. I was fortunate in my early training years to have the coaching of Don Ross, former Mr. America, who knew the value of shocking the muscle and who skillfully guided me in the right direction.

Preparing for a Mr. Olympia contest requires the highest training intensity. Because of the mental and physical drain I experience from such an ordeal, I find I must take one or two weeks off from weight training after the show. During the layoff, I increase my aerobic activities, such as bike riding, running, swimming, etc. The cessation of weight training allows the body to regenerate itself, thus making another cycle of growth possible.

TRAINING INTENSITY

When I was training for the 1980 Mr. Olympia, I worked out so hard I actually burst blood vessels in both eyeballs. Last year I learned to work just below that level of intensity, and I made outstanding progress. Training intensity increases naturally as you get stronger and bigger. It takes deliberate, conscious restraint to keep from overdoing it.

In 1980, the day of the Mr. Olympia contest, I weighed 195 pounds. Six weeks before the 1981 Mr. Olympia I weighed 215, ripped! And I had this long period of grace to play with details before the actual competition.

The previous year I didn't know how much was too much. This time I knew. I had learned from experience. I won't make the mistake of breaking blood vessels again. It takes a great deal of control to train properly. Violent, massive, reckless effort is not the answer.

SLOW, CONTINUOUS MOVEMENTS

When I'm in heavy training (e.g., 650-pound Squats, 400-pound Bench Presses, 600-pound Deadlifts—all of them for reps), I occasionally experience joint stress of varying degrees. When this occurs, I have found that I can still train with maximum intensity even though I am sometimes forced to lower the poundages on the exercises. Quite often, by using a medium-heavy weight, and the Slow, Continuous Tension and the Peak Contraction techniques, I am able to take the stress off the joint while keeping the load on the working muscle.

Don't misunderstand. I am not telling you to avoid heavy poundages. *You have to train intensely.* But I believe I have found a way to prevent the excessive stress on joints that causes injuries. The secret is: cycle your training poundages to match your mental and physical ups and downs.

Here's the way I incorporate this into my own training: when I work a particular body part, say, twice a week, one of those workouts will be heavy, the other medium-heavy. Occasionally, I will employ Slow, Continuous Tension movements on the lighter day. By using this technique, you can actually make a medium-heavy weight seem very heavy while helping to reduce joint stress and mental fatigue.

THE MIND

I must mention the importance of the mind. I feel it's by far the most important body part. It's amazing what you can accomplish when your mind is in tune with your body. Initially, a person develops a desire for training. Next, he develops a need to train. Finally, he is consumed by the need to succeed. What I am saying is this: if you expect to fail, you will fail. If you expect success, chances are you will succeed.

Your destiny in bodybuilding is determined by your concentration on all facets of your training. Mind and muscle must be linked. I recently experienced a phenomenon while doing heavy Hack Squats. My training intensity and concentration were so complete, I seemed to enter another world. I felt spacey, sort of freed from the drag of gravity. The Hack Squats felt as effortless as walking. I got off the machine and left the gym feeling I had been in another realm. I think I could call it a religious experience. I remember Arnold describing how he felt his biceps filling the room as he worked them, or Frank Zane painlessly watching himself train from a position outside his body. To these experiences I can now add my own.

Training intensity is vital to building a championship physique. But intensity to the point of injury is not the way to go. Cycling your training poundages as I've described is the answer.

Peaking

by Mike Mentzer

Muscles rebuilding, cells dividing, the human body is in a constant state of flux. And I am not referring to changes that occur from day to day or month to month, but those that take place moment to moment.

This is the result of the myriad stresses, both external and internal, that impinge on us from before we were born to the moment we die. Such widely divergent things as pain, work, heat, cold, poisons, loss of a loved one, studying for an exam, preparing for a physique contest, emotional conflict, and so on, ad infinitum, threaten to disrupt our internal makeup. Our pH balance, blood sugar level, electrolyte balance, hormone levels, and innumerable other complex processes are continually adapting to the wear and tear of life. This dynamic state also results in unceasing changes in our emotions, drives, impulses, sense of well-being, and our spiritual outlook.

Another feature of our existence that's important to us all, especially the bodybuilder, is the appearance of our bodies. The assertion that our physical appearance is subject to instant change will surprise many, since most of us think only of the changes we can induce over periods of days, weeks, months, and years—not hour to hour or moment to moment. It's true, of course, that the more dramatic changes in our appearance resulting from physical training and diet take place over longer stretches of time. Appreciable gains in mass take months at least. Even a 20-pound gain of muscle in one year—a tremendous gain, incidentally—amounts to less than an ounce a day, certainly not enough to be perceptible day to day. Losing fat and acquiring definition also takes time but is more noticeable on a daily basis, especially as we approach zero percent body fat.

Usually the day after a big physique contest there is a photo session for the winners and the runners-up. Invariably one or all of the participants are astonished at how much better they look and feel the day after the show. I have noticed this in myself. But how can you account for such an improvement after less than 24 hours?

As I said, our bodies are in a constant state of flux. It so happens that certain changes in our internal state alter certain aspects of our physical appearance almost the instant they occur. Some changes are dramatic enough to alter the appearance by as much as 50% for the better or the worse. Whether these changes add to or detract from our appearance depends on our awareness of them and ability to control them.

How well I remember a case where my ignorance of such factors caused my physique to change dramatically for the worse overnight. The night before I competed in the Mr. Universe contest in Acapulco in 1978, my girlfriend Cathy and I had dinner in a restaurant with Joe and Betty Weider. The evening fare featured seafood, which contains a certain amount of sodium. But the appetizer, as I recalled later, was particularly salty. Of course, salt makes you thirsty and our waiter made sure our water glasses were always filled. Needless to say I woke up on the morning of the biggest contest of my life waterlogged and devoid of most of the deep cuts I had had just the day before.

I didn't realize how bad I looked until Frank Zane, who was doing color commentary for CBS Sports, ran backstage after the Prejudging and asked what I had done to lose my cuts. Others made comments. The knowledge that I had gotten myself puffed up hurt my confidence going into the evening show. But luckily my shape, size, and symmetry were enough to give me the victory.

Had the competition been more keen, the outcome of that contest might have been different. Anyway, that near mishap taught me a lesson, one I have been able to put to good use.

Now, perhaps, you are beginning to get a better idea of how the appearance of the body can be altered in a matter of hours, or even minutes. Ever since my experience in Acapulco, I have studied this phenomenon intensely, keeping precise observations in my training journals and reading widely.

As bodybuilders, there are two major ways in which we improve our appearance: by adding muscle and by removing fat. Both take place over days, weeks, and months. The changes brought about through the addition of muscle and the loss of fat are usually of a gross nature in that they generally account for profound alternations in appearance.

I learned in my research, however, that the different amounts of salt in our tissues, along with fluid levels and blood volume, help determine how large and how cut up our muscles are. These factors are subject to fine tuning, and will determine whether or not a bodybuilder will be at his absolute peak condition on contest day. Being ignorant of these factors, or even making a small slipup, could make the difference between winning and losing.

Once you have done the groundwork (training hard and watching your diet) in preparation for a contest, you will want to go into the contest at your absolute biggest and ripped—in peak condition, in other words. The following suggestions will give you the fine-tune control over your appearance that you'll require to reach peak condition.

GIVE YOURSELF ADEQUATE TIME TO GET READY

Begin your contest preparation well enough in advance so that you will reach a peak condition—maximum muscle size with minimum body fat—at least a week in advance of the contest. During this preparation period, keep a training journal in which you maintain an accurate record of your body weight under various circumstances, such as before training, after training, upon arising, after posing practice, etc. This is especially important as you approach peak condition. Once you reach that peak, note your body weight and strive to maintain it with little fluctuation as you go into the contest. It's ridiculous to go into a contest still struggling to lose weight. Reaching that ideal condition a week or so before the show will give you much more fine-tune control.

CONTROL THE WATER LEVEL WITHIN YOUR BODY

Once you have reached a peak, where you have done all you reasonably could up to that point to build mass and lose fat, it's the amount of water in your body that will determine whether you go into the contest with large, pumped muscles and skin like cellophane, or flat, deflated muscles with puffy skin. The secret is knowing how to maintain optimum blood volume in the body and maximum fluid pressure within the muscle while simultaneously getting rid of all extra water under the skin. Even a normally hydrated person has more subcutaneous water than would be consistent with an absolute peak. It's imperative that you learn how to control the amount of water in your body and its distribution if you want to appear at your best on contest day. There are five ways you can control that amount of water in your body:

Sweating

While I have always known that sweating causes the body to lose water, it wasn't until my preparation for the 1979 Mr. Olympia that I learned how much water is contained subcutaneously, and how effective intensive sweating can be in getting rid of it. After each workout I would go onto the roof of my house. I would rub a light oil into my skin to cause my body to heat up more, especially in areas like my lower back and abdomen where I tend to hold more water. Within two hours I would have endured all the heat and perspiration I could stand.

Each and every day I did this, and each day I was astounded at how much water I lost from under my skin. Even more surprising was the effect this had on my appearance. Before the two hours of sweating, I appeared moderately cut and striated, but after the sweating my cuts appeared much deeper and I had striations that normally weren't visible. In addition, the skin all over my body would be a third as thick after the sweating. You'd be surprised to what extent water makes up what we suppose is fat.

But you must be careful not to overdo the sweating since you lose important minerals and electrolytes along with the water. Moreover, if your body heat goes too high, you can suffer heatstroke and even death. Losing too much body water this way can also detract from your appearance. Muscle tissue, remember, is comprised of more than 70% water, and the blood pumped into muscle to increase size is also made up mostly of water. So too much sweating can lower blood volume and decrease mass, if only temporarily.

Sweating should be used primarily the last week or two before the contest to help control subcutaneous water as well as help rid the body of excess salt, which holds water in the body. If the weather is not warm, saunas or running in a heavy sweatsuit can be substituted. Increase your potassium intake during periods of heavy sweating, but continue to restrict salt in your diet.

Limiting Salt and Water Intake

In addition to, or instead of sweating, the limiting of salt and water in your diet for up to two days before the contest can increase your definition as well.

The best way to restrict your salt is buy a book that lists the sodium level of foods and eliminate the foods that are heavy in salt. One part sodium holds 180 parts water in the body!

You can reduce your sodium intake for several

days leading up to the contest, but reducing your intake of water should be limited to no more than two days before the show. And note that I say *reduce* your water intake, not eliminate it. Remember again that the amount of water in the muscle, as well as in the blood, determines, in part, muscle size and the ability to pump.

So play it by ear. If you are particularly puffy, cut your normal intake of water and fluids by two-thirds. When you're thirsty, drink one-third of what you would usually take in.

I did this the day before the 1979 Mr. Olympia and noted a steady increase in my definition and a decrease in my skin thickness. As Prejudging approached, I increased my water intake a bit since I knew it would be murderously hot under the lights. I was ripped and my skin was tight by then, so I knew a little water increase wouldn't hurt and would actually help in pumping up the muscles and keeping my energy up.

Diuretics

The measures I have described above for thinning the skin and ridding the body of water be controlled by the individual, and they work extremely well either by themselves or together. There's no good reason for a bodybuilder to take diuretics before the show. Diuretics are unpredictable and can cause you to lose too much water. And since body fat is made up of only 15% water while muscle is more than 70% water, most of the water will come from the muscle and blood. This will deflate the muscles, reduce pumpability, and absolutely wipe out vascularity. The potassium loss that results will cause weakness and shakiness. Diuretics are radical expedients and can cause the loss of up to *eight pounds* in a matter of hours. And the resulting electrolyte imbalance could take days to restore.

Ketosis

The ketone bodies that enter the blood when fat is being burned cause increased urination as a means of ridding the body of the ketones. I usually try to stay in ketosis by keeping my calories low and activity high right up to the night before the contest. Ketostix, available in any drugstore, can be used to monitor ketone levels. I advise that you don't stay in heavy (or purple) ketosis, since that is a sign that you have used up all your body's glycogen.

Activity and Metabolic Increase

Inactivity causes circulation to slow down and retards elimination. This is detrimental to the bodybuilder about to compete, since water and salts accumulate in the tissues. If you tend to wind down going into a contest, don't just lie around and stay on the same diet, even if it's a restricted one. The decreased activity will cause you to burn fewer calories and eliminate wastes less rapidly. Aerobic activities like running or biking will keep circulation optimal and prevent wastes, salts, and water from accumulating in the body. The night before the Olympia, I ran for 30 minutes and I firmly believe it helped me attain the peak I had the next day.

GLYCOGEN LEVELS

Carbohydrates are essential in the bodybuilder's diet since they provide the fuel the body requires for high-intensity muscular contraction. In addition to supplying energy, carbohydrate in the form of glycogen (a string of glucose molecules stuck together) is stored in the muscle, where each gram of glycogen stores three grams of water. People who go on very low- or zero-carbohydrate diets often marvel at the immediate and dramatic loss of weight that results. Losses of 10–15 pounds the first week are common. Such losses are mostly due to the body eliminating water, not fat. (The loss of three pounds of fat a week is the most you can hope for.) Much of this water comes from the muscle. As the body uses the stored glycogen in the muscle for energy due to the absence of dietary carbohydrate, the water molecules that were attached to the glycogen will pass out of the muscle and then out of the body.

Any intelligent bodybuilder would not go on a low-carb diet even if he or she is trying to lose fat. As long as the daily calorie intake is below maintenance levels you will lose fat. The best way to lose fat is on a reduced calorie diet comprised of 60% carbohydrate, 25% protein, and 15% fat. Even on such a moderate- to high-carbohydrate diet, the muscles will not store much glycogen as long as the calories are below maintenance levels. To restore glycogen to the fullest possible levels within your muscles so they'll swell and take on a tremendous pump, keep your diet the same and reduce your overall activity levels the last two days before the show so you don't burn the carbohydrates immediately for energy. Or keep your activity level constant and just increase your daily calorie intake so it's closer to maintenance levels.

Now, I'm not suggesting that you go out and eat every carbohydrate in sight. Once you have filled the glycogen stores in your muscles completely, any excess can cause water to "spill" into the subcutaneous space and cause you to appear puffy. This seems to be especially true if you're on steroids.

VOLUME OF FOOD EATEN

It's vital that you don't stuff yourself those last days before a show. Eating to excess will cause your stomach to protrude and will slow down the normal rate of elimination, causing wastes, salts, and water to accumulate in the body. By keeping your bowels relatively empty, you speed up the transit time of food through the intestines. And, of course, the importance of keeping your gut small and tight cannot be overemphasized.

BLOOD PACKING

Once the word got out a few years back that athletes from various fields of endeavor were using blood packing (taking transfusions of nutrient-laden plasma) to enhance performance, it was inevitable that bodybuilders would try it. Some of them thought that blood packing would increase muscle size and enhance vascularity. While that might work, the body would soon detect the abnormal blood volume and restore the normal level by speeding up urination. Such a practice would also be very hazardous, so please forget it!

PUMPING

Increasing muscular size and enhancing vascularity by the selective redistribution of blood volume has been practiced by bodybuilders for decades and, of course, is known as pumping. Since our blood supply is limited, don't try to pump every part of your body before going onstage. Pump only your two weakest body parts for no more than 15 minutes before going onstage. A muscle can be over-pumped, wiping out the cuts and definition of that body part. Pump the muscle just enough to round it out and bring the veins to the surface. Perform light movements in rapid succession when pumping up. Overpumping can also cause fatigue and shakiness onstage, so don't overdo it.

STEROIDS

Small doses of steroids the last several weeks before a contest help maintain size and vascularity. Oral anabolics in particular often cause puffiness. Any oral anabolic steroid you might be taking should be eliminated entirely the last week while injectables should be reduced in dosage the last two weeks. This reduction in steroids the last two weeks should not adversely affect muscle size if this size is not merely the result of pumping. Reducing the steroid level in your body will aid tremendously in controlling water levels and definition.

Attaining an absolute peak on a predetermined day is an art. Very few bodybuilders ever master it, as evidenced by the incredibly low rate of consistency even among professional bodybuilders. Only through experience and the awareness of the above factors can you ever hope to come close. Those who take the time and energy to master contest peaking will dominate the sport.

Weight Training Made Safe

by Lou Ferrigno

When proper safety procedures are followed, weight training and bodybuilding are totally safe recreational and physical fitness activities. But when safety rules are ignored, chances are you can hurt yourself—sometimes seriously.

Perhaps you don't believe me. If so, here's a brief sampling of injury reports received at the *Muscle & Fitness* editorial offices recently:

NEW YORK—An experienced 30-year-old male bodybuilder was found dead on a pressing bench in his basement, a 330-pound barbell resting across his neck. Apparently he had blacked out while doing a heavy Bench Press and the bar had crashed down across his neck, rupturing his larynx and strangling him.

CALIFORNIA—A lightly built and inexperienced junior high school boy was lifting weights during his lunch hour. The weight room was crowded and unsupervised, and the floor littered with weights. After an incomplete warm-up, the boy tried to lift 100 pounds (his limit) in the Military Press. The barbell pulled him backward as he finished the Press, and when he tried to step back to regain his balance he tripped over a barbell on the floor. He fell on his back and the barbell he'd been using crashed across his face. His jaw and cheek bones were smashed and numerous teeth knocked out. Eventually he had to undergo reconstructive surgery. His total medical bills came to more than $7,000.

FLORIDA—A powerful young woman bodybuilder with competitive aspirations was squatting with 225 pounds, nearly 100 pounds more than her body weight. On the final rep of her set, she began to stall out halfway up from the bottom position. Fearing that she would be pinned under the barbell, she leaned her torso forward to get better leverage so she could finish the repetition. Just before completing the rep she felt a sharp popping sensation in the middle of her back. A moment later she bent over to pick up a light barbell and was unable to straighten up. Her poor biomechanical (body) position in the Squat had resulted in a ruptured spinal disc. Following corrective surgery, she has only a 50–50 chance of ever again being able to train for bodybuilding competition. Her medical bills and physical therapy expenses have totaled nearly $10,000.

MICHIGAN—A 20-year-old man with limited weight-training experience played several games of racquetball at his YMCA and then decided to do some Bench Presses to finish off his workout. His racquetball partner said he was going to call it a day and went off to take his shower. So the 20-year-old worked out alone. Bench pressing 150 pounds, he blacked out and the bar fell across his neck, cutting off the flow of blood to his brain, but causing no other injury. Sometime later a person passing through the weight room removed the barbell from the man's neck. The man survived, but he suffered considerable brain damage since his brain had been deprived of oxygen for so long.

Admittedly, these are isolated cases, but several deaths *have* occurred during weight training sessions, and thousands of weight training injuries—most minor, but some serious—are incurred every year. Ironically, almost all these deaths and injuries could have been prevented if proper weight training safety procedures were followed. But, unfortunately, very few weight-training books even mention safety, even fewer magazine articles discuss the subject, and far too few weight-training instructors place proper emphasis on safety.

As a service to the readers of *Muscle & Fitness*, I am offering the following 12 rules of weight-training and bodybuilding safety. If you follow these safety rules, you will probably never experience a weight-related injury. I personally have received several joint and muscle injuries participating in other sports, but have never been injured in 15 years of bodybuilding training. So I know how well these rules work.

Use Spotters

Always have a spotter or two on hand when you're using heavy weights in the basic exercises, particularly the Bench Press and Squat. An alert spotter stationed at the head of the bench could have prevented the two Bench Pressing accidents mentioned earlier. All a spotter would have had to do was quickly pull up the bar when it began to stall out or actually descend. A spotter at each end of the bar probably would have prevented the squatting accident mentioned earlier, too. Instead of rounding her back, the young woman could have merely said, "Take it," and the spotters would have immediately removed the bar, preventing the injury.

Spotters are seldom necessary when you're doing dumbbell movements; obviously, it's difficult to be pinned under two dumbbells. And you'll never need a spotter when exercising on weight machines. Despite the expense drawback of most of these machines, one advantage they have is that you can't be pinned under them while doing an exercise.

Never Train Alone

Most weight-training and bodybuilding injuries and accidents occur when someone is training alone. So a hard and fast safety rule is: never train alone, even in your home gym. Cultivate a training partner or two. Such partners not only can spot you on heavy exercises, but will be able to provide moral support and help you with forced reps.

Use Catch Racks

Many Squat racks have either numerous sets of heavy pins sticking out from angled supports or a pair of horizontal bars on which you can drop a weight when you begin to get stuck in a Squat. These catch racks can help prevent back injuries such as the one incurred by the young woman mentioned earlier.

Use Collars

Regardless of how inconvenient this might sometimes seem, always use collars to secure the plates. I once saw a bodybuilder squatting with 450 pounds on the bar, but no collars. On his last rep one end of the bar dipped. Slowly five 45-pound plates fell off. The other end of the barbell—now suddenly very heavy by comparison—whipped downward, dumping its plates. This motion of the bar strained the bodybuilder's shoulder and lower back. The injury would not have happened if he'd taken a few seconds to put collars on the barbell before squatting.

Never Hold Your Breath During an Exercise

There's a tendency to hold one's breath while lifting very heavy weights, particularly in the Bench Press. This causes what is scientifically called a Valsalva Effect, which results in such great intrathoracic pressure that it hinders veinous return of blood from the brain, causing a blackout. In a Bench Press that can be disastrous. Get into the habit of rhythmically breathing in and out on all exercises. And if you find it difficult to breathe during a maximum effort, simply grunting or groaning during a rep will open the throat's glottis (breathing passage) enough to prevent the Valsalva Effect and the resulting blackout.

Maintain Good Gym Housekeeping

Someone in the gym should always be assigned the task of regularly replacing barbells, dumbbells, and loose plates in the proper racks. The best rule to follow is for each bodybuilder to replace his or her own weights as soon as a set has been completed. If the weights had been replaced like this, the young man doing the Military Press probably would not have had his face smashed.

Train under Competent Supervision

If at all possible, always train in a weight room or gym that has a knowledgeable instructor or coach constantly in attendance. This will prevent horseplay that can lead to accidents. Also, a good instructor can spot and correct mistakes in training form and procedure. Such competent instruction will prevent many injuries, even years in advance, by instilling proper exercise habits and body positions.

Don't Train in an Overcrowded Gym

If you are forced to wait for more than 2–3 minutes to use a particular piece of equipment, the gym in which you're training is too crowded and you should try to schedule your workouts when it's less crowded. Waiting too long between sets will allow your body to cool down and leave you susceptible to injuries.

Always Warm Up Thoroughly

You must always warm up for at least 5–10 minutes with calisthenics, or stretching, jogging, and jumping rope, before beginning your weight-training session. And if you're using very heavy weights in a basic exercise, always be sure to do 2–3 light, but progressively heavier, warm-up sets of that movement before tackling your heaviest poundages. A warm-up not only makes muscles, joints, and tendons resistant to injury, but also refines neuromuscular coordination in any weight-training movement. If you immediately went to your maximum weight in a Military Press, your coordination would be very poor. But after a warm-up it would be much better. Lack of a proper warm-up and, therefore, insufficient neuromuscular coordination is one reason why the boy doing the Military Press lost his balance and was injured.

Use Proper Biomechanical Positions in All Exercises

In each weight-training exercise there are body positions that *must always* be maintained if you are to avoid injury. For example, anyone who has walked through a factory or warehouse has seen signs pointing out that the hips should be kept low and the back flat when lifting a weight from the floor, and that most of the lifting should be done with the legs. This is exactly the biomechanical position you must use when lifting a barbell from the floor in a Deadlift or Power Clean. And in the Squat, the spine must never be allowed to round forward. These and other correct biomechanical positions for exercises are constantly stressed in *Muscle & Fitness*, and in the many weight-training and bodybuilding books on the market. Pay very close attention to these suggested body positions. Concentrate on them in your training. Don't let your mind wander when you're doing an exercise. It's when your concentration breaks that an injury can occur.

Use a Lifting Belt

Several types of weightlifting belts are advertised in each issue of *Muscle & Fitness.* Buy one and use it for all Squats, Overhead Presses, and for all back exercises done in a bent-over position. Heavy leather lifting belts protect both your lower back and abdomen from injuries.

Acquire as Much Knowledge as Possible about Weight Training and Bodybuilding

The more you know about this sport, the less likely you are to become injured. So read every article in *Muscle & Fitness,* and try to build up an extensive library of weight-training, bodybuilding, nutrition, anatomy, kinesiology, and physiology books. Read them as often as possible to acquire an expert's knowledge of bodybuilding. The more you know, the less your chances of injury.

Roy Callender wears a lifting belt before doing heavy Squats.

The Mechanics of Squats

by Joe Weider

Ask anyone experienced in weight training which exercise he considers the best of all, and chances are he'll tell you the Squat. It has been the traditional answer for decades, ever since the beginning of modern weight training. We have always written about the importance of Squats as the basic exercise for creating muscular mass, gaining body weight, developing overall strength, and increasing power.

Yet, the training philosophies of the late arrivals on the fitness scene tend to shove Squats in the corner or eliminate them altogether. Too many of those magnificent health spas have minimal barbell squatting facilities. The Nautilus clubs depend on machines for leg work, but machine Leg Presses are not the same as Squats.

The Squat has become a lost art, except among a few strength specialists. The lift has been dropped, partly through misconceptions of what Squats do to you. As for the Squat widening the hips, that is simply an anatomical impossibility. The muscles that are the prime movers in the Squat are situated posteriorly and anteriorly on the skeleton. The pelvis itself is a fixed structure, incapable of expanding laterally under normal exercise pressures.

The Squat, more than any other weight-training exercise, forces the body to grow. Squats can increase the total muscle volume of the body, reduce the percentage of body fat, and increase overall muscular strength. They are the requisite for reaching one's full bodybuilding potential. All the top bodybuilders have used the Squat as a base for building their bodies. Among the powerlifting athletes, the Squat itself is perhaps the most representative of their sport, requiring keen technique and brute strength. When they go after a record, powerlifters concentrate more on Squats than on either of the other two required lifts, the Bench Press and Deadlift. The powerlifters' super-heavyweight class Squat record is now more than 1,000 pounds. Extreme muscular mass as well as definition have become the distinguishing marks of the modern powerlifters. Through ingenuity, advanced techniques, and surefire methods of reducing body weight while gaining strength, they have gained a quality of muscle in recent years that has alerted bodybuilders to the possibilities in their methods.

Three years ago, Tom Platz burst upon the international bodybuilding scene with astonishing leg development. He had always done loads of Squats. However, his upper body was no match for his lower body, and as a result he found the going tough during the subsequent years. During the past year he took another tack. Rather than try to balance his proportions by

Bertil Fox demonstrates mechanics of squat.

easing up on his leg work, Tom intensified his Squat training on the assumption that his upper body would benefit. Of course, he was right. At the 1981 Mr. Olympia contest, Platz's legs were more sensational than ever, and on top of it his upper body had acquired a muscular mass that compared with the best in the game. He came very close to winning.

The Squat has been dominant in the training of three-time Mr. Olympia Frank Zane. During the first part of his career Frank's thighs were disproportionately large. Even later when he trained with Arnold, the two superstars regularly used 400 pounds for reps on their Squats. Zane continues to squat regularly and considers that part of his training essential to his overall development. He thoroughly prepares for each squatting session and does each rep with slow precision. He is careful not to awaken his dormant back and knee injuries. He uses powerlifting superwraps, putting them on his knees before each set and taking them off during rests between the sets to allow for full circulation. He keeps his trunk as erect as possible both during his slow descent and strong ascent. He uses the progressive resistance method, starting with a light warm-up and increasing poundages on subsequent sets, 8–10 reps on each set. He exerts full power on the final high poundage for the full set of 8–10 reps, a system presently popular with record-breaking powerlifters. Zane's is a very careful performance, representative of the kind of training done by today's top bodybuilders. For his latest professional contests Zane resorted to certain training techniques used by elite powerlifters. For a period he actually trained with them.

The same power-building methods that helped Zane increase his overall size after two decades of training can work for any bodybuilder. The Squat is fundamental to building a better body. Most bodybuilders are aware of this fact, yet too few are aware of the Squat techniques so important in keeping tissues intact while extracting the most benefit from the effort. If their goal is to have the ultimately developed body, it's due time that bodybuilders learn all there is to know about squatting. They should take time out to learn these techniques and then apply them methodically and regularly. It is imperative for the advanced bodybuilder whose spectrum of possibilities for progress has drastically narrowed. Proper and safe techniques for handling maximum poundages with maximum effort remain the basis of progressive bodybuilding.

The study of Squat techniques is intriguing. It has always been a challenging lift, and more than any other exercise bodybuilders will boast of their Squat capability. Squat strength is a fair measure of their overall condition.

In his articles on the biomechanics of the Squat appearing in *Powerlifting USA* magazine, researcher Tom McLaughlin, Ph.D., Director of the Biomechanics Laboratory at Auburn University, describes existing research studies on the Squat. In a "kinematic" study, the displacements, velocities, and accelerations of the Squat motion were analyzed and comparisons made between high-skilled and low-skilled squatters. In a "kinetic" study, muscular forces and external forces affecting the Squat motion were studied. Patterns of muscular involvement that characterize a great Squat were sought.

It was discovered in these two studies that the vertical velocity of the bar and pattern of motion were the same among all high-skilled squatters regardless of their body weight and maximum weight capability. It was found that techniques between the high-skilled and low-skilled squatters differed remarkably:

- During the first 6–10 inches of descent into the Squat position, the high-skilled squatters lowered the bar slower for better control.
- The bar was moving at a higher velocity when it reached the parallel Squat position for the low-skilled squatters, thus causing more bounce at the bottom of the movement than for the better squatters.
- The high-skilled squatters leaned forward less and kept the knees from moving forward as much during the bar's descent than the low-skilled squatters.
- In coming up from the bottom position, the low-skilled squatters leaned forward more and let the hips come out backward more than the high-skilled squatters.

The bodybuilder should check himself against these differences and attempt to emulate the performance technique of the high-skilled squatter. These studies were made between many of powerlifting's world class squatters and less skilled lifters competing in the same event. The velocity and performance patterns were found to be strikingly similar in studies among the high-skilled squatters in many subsequent national and world powerlifting meets.

The bodybuilder relies a lot on instinctive training to iron out his flaws. This has always been a reliable and effective method of training. Through trial and error and a sufficient period of time, the most satisfactory technique for the individual evolves. However, the bodybuilder cannot give the Squat the time, attention, and effort that the powerlifter can. Hence, flaws in the bodybuilder's Squat training may persist, limiting the benefits.

Collectively the best squatters have stumbled upon the best patterns in technique through their own trial and error. Research has proved that their patterns are identical. Obviously, there is only one way to squat—the proven way. For the bodybuilder, if he will take the time to patiently practice these Squat techniques, this is a bonanza, a sure way to overcome sticking points in size, strength, and muscularity. Admittedly there will always be certain individuals of unusual anatomical or mental makeups that permit them to deviate from proven patterns of technique and still be successful. It would be to the advantage of most athletes to use the advanced techniques with all the common factors that the best squatters use.

In his initial studies, McLaughlin also discovered that the sticking point for all squatters comes in the same position, regardless of the lifter's body size or the weight of the bar. This seems to be a point where the angle between the thighs and the lower legs is about 30 degrees. Failure to make a lift will invariably happen there, which means the squatter must train in a way that prevents him from getting stuck at that point.

It was also shown that the high-skilled lifters had greater momentum than those of lesser ability going through the sticking point. They tended to generate more speed and position themselves more favorably by the time they reached the sticking point.

The serious bodybuilder ought to know his anatomy. Much of bodybuilding exercising is based on isolating a body part so that the muscles in that area are forced to take on the workload imposed on it. Common kinesiological studies of muscle activity correctly name muscles largely involved in such highly specific exercises as Arm Curls, Presses, Calf Raises, Leg Curls, Leg Extensions, or Sit-Ups. Those are simple movements. The more complex muscular involvement in the Squat movement is harder to define. McLaughlin's studies have identified some common factors in technique that were mostly the result of empirical experience among the lifters.

Says McLaughlin: "What this means is that research has hardly begun to fully answer our many questions regarding muscular involvement in the variety of exercises we perform in our training. It is entirely conceivable that a majority of each of our workouts is in large part wasted effort, that is, working muscles not of major importance."

From a bodybuilding standpoint this might suggest that multiple sets of the many different exercises for the various body parts are wasted effort. Perhaps this means that we can better tap our potential with a heavy-duty exercise such as the Squat. The other exercises for specific body parts might be supplemental movements. The Squat builds the all-around power and size that elicit greater response from the other exercises. In other words, it's not important that we do 20 sets of exercises for the biceps when we can get the same result from 10 sets catalyzed by Squat training. No one is yet sure why Squats impart this overall potential, so it remains a highly intriguing area of research.

In the kinetic analyses of McLaughlin's research, calculating what are called "resultant muscular torques," the sum of the effects of all the muscles acting on the thighs and trunk during squatting was determined. The torques told to what extent and when the major muscle groups were involved during the Squat. There were both obvious and nonobvious results.

It was obvious that, for the trunk torques, the back extensor muscles were involved the most during the entire Squat, and the torque increased more as the lifter leaned forward. For the thigh torque, greatest involvement of the quadriceps occurred in the very low Squat position.

Among the nonobvious results, it was found that the magnitude of the trunk torque did not increase in direct proportion to the increase in the amount of weight used and the body weight of the subject. As the weights got heavier, the back extensor involvement of the high-skilled lifters was less than that of the less-skilled lifters. This was partly the result of the high-skilled lifters keeping the trunk more vertical. The high-skilled lifters also tended to use the thigh extensors more. This prescribes a technique that more fully involves the quadriceps, with comparatively less involvement of the back extensors. Faulty technique, excessive forward lean, would detract from the effect of the exercise on the quadriceps.

Since the greatest torque was always that of the back extensor, it would be reasonable to avoid any other form of lower back work on the day of the Squat workout, or to avoid the Squat itself when one is excessively tired or possibly experiencing low back pain.

More extensive studies are needed, of course, but it is obvious that the Squat involves other major muscle groups such as the gluteals, hamstrings, and calves.

When our magazine was *Muscle Power* we ran many articles on powerlifting techniques, starting in the late 1960s. Many of the original Squat principles are still valid, but through the years much more has been learned. Certain general rules can be derived from all the years of hit-and-miss technical analysis on the Squat by powerlifters. Training Editor Ron Fernando of *Powerlifting USA* magazine has compiled a comparative study of high-skilled squatter styles, and bodybuilders can advantageously apply these techniques to their own Squat training.

First of all, you have to closely evaluate your physique to determine if a wide, medium, or narrow stance should be taken. An extremely wide squatting stance has been phased out in favor of a more moderate-to-wide stance. The descent should be controlled, slow for the first 6–10 inches of descent. Excessive use of the lower back can be a deterrent to ultimate Squat power. Well-developed abdominals help ensure a more upright position during the descent. Proper use of the power belt also helps.

The philosophy of sets and reps has changed from the early days when the 5–4–3–2–1 reps system was in vogue. This system did not build much muscle size, however. Then came the five-sets-of-five-reps system for building bulk, but the energy expenditure on individual sets was unequal and seldom maximum. The more popular system today is a sort of inverted pyramid, progressive resistance warm-up with low reps until the top weight is reached, then doing an all-out, high-intensity set of eight reps. In this way most of the energy is saved for the maximum crucial set. Bodybuilders have generally always used the five-sets-of-10-reps system for Squats. This also prevented maximum energy output on a high poundage since the bodybuilders had used most of their energy on the previous sets. It may be worthwhile for the bodybuilder to try an energy-saving system using progressive reps and progressive poundages, doing perhaps 2–5 reps on the first four sets, increasing the weight with each subsequent set, and doing eight high-intensity reps on the fifth set with a top weight. This system makes sense because it seems to preclude any point of diminishing returns.

The time has come to place more emphasis on technique to get the most benefit from Squat training. Energy conservation is the keynote. The idea is to get maximum muscular response with the least energy output, thus conserving the energy necessary for the vital recuperative process during the three or four days between Squat sessions. In addition, stretching should be given a more important role, mainly for the prevention of injury.

Years ago, powerlifters found that when they wore blue jeans they were able to squat better. The denim material became bound tightly around the thighs and knees during descent, creating a buildup of elastic energy that was released during ascent and catapulted the lifter out of the low position. The concept has evolved today to special suits, wraps, and belts. Researcher McLaughlin points to evidence that a good deal of energy in human motion is saved by elastic structures in the body. In one study it was shown that squatters used up to 27% less energy when using a slight rebound at the

bottom of a Squat rather than stopping dead for a moment. In addition the upward force is increased up to 30%.

Reports McLaughlin: "The mechanism by which this phenomenon occurs is when a muscle is stressed (descending in the Squat), and almost immediately before the muscle shortens (starting the ascent) there will be more energy available to the upward motion. (This follows the classic characteristic that a muscle exerts its greatest contractile force from a state of full extension.) This means there will be more weight lifted in the Squat. In other words, one needs a counter movement followed almost immediately by the movement desired. Hence a rebound at the bottom of the Squat is very helpful in getting more weight lifted. There is an optimal amount of speed in this bounce at the bottom of the Squat that each lifter should use."

For most bodybuilders at present this must be determined through personal practice.

Top lifters begin to increase the velocity of descent at a point a few inches above parallel. This permits a more moderate rebound. Training helps increase the ability to store and retrieve elastic energy. This energy is stored in the tendons and in the elastic components of the muscles themselves. In the early 1950s we wrote about the Weider Rebound Principle using bodybuilder Leroy Colbert as the subject. The purpose was to handle more weight to more quickly increase muscle mass and strength.

Squatting authority Pete Vuono, in an article on lifting attire (*Powerlifting USA*—June 1981), feels that wraps and suits, properly fitted so as not to cut off circulation or cut into the skin, can help prevent injuries as well as offer moral and physical support.

Many top squatters wear lightweight shoes with heels from 1–1.5 inches for better balance. For the bodybuilder placing the heels on a board of the same thickness would suffice, a practice that has been in existence a long time. A couple of pairs of thick socks help to promote more leverage and upward thrust during rebound.

Vuono recommends a lifting belt 10 centimeters (3.9 inches) wide, which helps keep your trunk upright and helps the squeeze effect in getting out of a deep Squat. The belt should be worn fairly low on the hips.

According to Vuono, knee wraps should always be worn when squatting. Knee injury can mean the end of a career because, short of surgery, it is generally irreparable. Prevention is the best cure. Vuono suggests wearing knee wraps snug to protect rather than tight to act as an aid. Since bodybuilders aren't shooting for records, wraps should be worn snug, not tight. Removing the wraps between sets and massaging the knees helps maintain good circulation.

Learn to wrap properly. Start wrapping just below the knee. Wrap in a crisscross manner to prevent the wrap from moving or bunching up. Just above the kneecap lay on several wraps, one on top of the other for added support.

Lifting suits can enhance-limit attempt Squats. It seems wiser not to depend on them for general bodybuilding Squat training.

To prevent the bar from slipping down your back from sweat and to prevent the knurling from cutting into your skin, always wear a shirt when you squat.

The bar should rest on the shoulders about an inch below the deltoids for best balance, depending on your personal structure, of course. Holding the bar at that position may cause considerable wrist strain, in which case it would be wise to also wrap the wrists snugly.

Squat training should be done twice a week, both during the off-season and when training for competition. Squat sessions should be at least 72 hours apart. You will need that much time for full recuperation. One of the semiweekly workouts may consist of pause Squats with more moderate weights, holding each rep in the low position for a long count. Use the aforementioned energy-saving pyramid system, increasing the poundage with successive low-reps sets and then doing a high-intensity final set of eight reps. The second workout may consist of regular Squats without the pause, using somewhat heavier weights.

By keeping the Squat training poundages at a fairly intense effort level all the time, it is easier to shift to the mass- and strength-building higher poundages you will want to use during those 4–8-week cycles of heavy training that are recommended two or three times during the year.

Strict Style is Still King!

by Chris Dickerson

The weights are my tools. I build my physique with them. My general philosophy on training is that the weights are there to serve me. I am not in the business of fighting weights. I am not a slave to their demands. I am the boss.

My method of training is based on strict form, peak contraction, and sustained tension. When I struggle to complete the final rep of a set, I like to think I'm "squeezing out" the last bit of effort. I believe my method is a refinement of the Weider Forced Reps Principle.

I use moderately heavy weights that allow me to perform movements in strict form. I like to concentrate on the actual contraction of the muscle during the entire range of motion. When I reach the top position of an exercise, I hold the weight for a second or two at maximum tension and then release for the slow return movement.

You don't get size just by using heavy weights. What determines muscularity and development is proper training—strict style and concentration. The mind plays a very important part in developing muscle, and you cannot concentrate if you're putting all your effort into just getting the weight up.

In the short intervals between sets I make use of the Iso-Tension Principle, continually flexing the muscles I have worked to keep the blood flowing in them. You have to be concerned with getting blood into the area. Flexing also helps to develop contractile force, educating the nervous system to fire more stimuli into the muscles. Flexing plays a major role in muscle development and should be practiced to the fullest.

When I do an exercise, it may take me 3–4 seconds to raise the weight, and even longer for the return movement. By definition, strict movements take longer.

My training methods revolve around concentration. I don't even like to have a training partner. A partner is good if you're doing heavy powerlifting exercises, and I will use heavy weights on such lifts as the Bench Press, Deadlift, and Squat. In bodybuilding training, however, I like to get inside my body. That means *concentrating.* People are seldom on the same wavelength. I prefer to "feel" the weights in my own way. I don't appreciate someone exhorting me to greater effort. It distracts me. I consider it outside interference. I am a professional who—by now—knows his own capabilities.

During a workout I am in a steady state of awareness. I am communicating with my body. I tend to lose that contact if I use very heavy weights because my chief concern then becomes lifting the weight, not developing my body.

While I'm working out, I often visualize what my body is going to look like. I remember something Ray Mentzer wrote regarding visualization. He said that in order to stimulate his imagination in the gym he even thought about heroic comic book characters. Well, I don't take it to that extent, but visualization is an important part of my training.

I have reached a state of development that can be improved only by refinement. My training is slanted toward refinement—density, cuts, definition, and peak development. My present method of training is best for the muscular qualities I need to compete at the professional level.

The beginner should compromise to some extent. He should not use such heavy weights that they tend to stress the joints and tendons more than the muscles. The beginner should use weights that he can handle correctly. If he's doing cheating movements—a powerful, advanced training system—he should be aware that he is using that system and not simply making a random effort to lift a lot of weight. He should know that the Cheating Principle does not work well even for the advanced bodybuilder if too much weight is used.

The problem with cheating, especially for the beginner, is that it becomes a habit. When it comes time not to cheat, you may think you're using strict form, but you're not; you're still cheating. I think the beginner has a better chance of getting mass by increasing his calorie intake than by the slipshod use of heavy weights.

After you have reached a bodyweight compatible with your bone structure and height, you can adopt the methods I use. I truly believe you can't totally refine your physique without using my methods.

One thing, however, I don't separate the muscularity and refinement from the development. I treat them much the same. When I first began training under Bill Pearl, I would handle as much weight as I could but in very strict style, even in the Squat. When I went home after those workouts, I drank certified raw milk, and ate peanut butter, bananas, raisins, and dates. I consumed enough calories to make it possible for me to handle heavy weights in the next workout. It takes calories to build muscle mass and strength. After 19 years of bodybuilding, I have come to the conclusion that size and definition are determined by diet, not by training methods.

I aim for 12 repetitions on most exercises. For the beginner I would suggest 10 reps. I do three exercises of six sets each per body part, a total of 18 sets. I may also do two flushing sets of 15–20 reps. That's a lot of work for one body part, but I only work that hard as a contest approaches. In normal training I prefer to do 12 sets per body part with slightly heavier weights, and I don't diet as strictly.

For a five-year period prior to my return to competitive bodybuilding in late 1979, I worked heavy, doing about eight reps—but always in the strictest form. Doing fewer reps (say, five) would not have been sufficient to get a high volume of blood into the muscle. I was working heavier, but my diet made it possible. When you're dieting strictly, you have to make do with the rationed fuel. Since I was consuming more calories, I could work heavier, although it didn't seem heavier. A 35-pound dumbbell when you're dieting feels heavier than a 55-pound dumbbell when you're not.

I believe vitamins and minerals are particularly important when you're training for competition. Before a contest, when you're taking in a limited amount of natural food, you need supplements to give you energy and drive. It's difficult to tell exactly what vitamins, minerals, and supplements do for you, but there is proof that when you're training hard, your immune system begins to weaken due to the physical stress; thus, you become vulnerable to debilitating ailments. It has been shown that athletes who take vitamins, minerals, and supplements during hard training have a lower incidence of these ailments.

As a bodybuilder gets older, I think vitamin and mineral supplements become even more important. Bodybuilders make far greater demands on their bodies than the average person; consequently, they need more of the supportive elements.

In summary, the core of my training method is tension, flexing, concentration, and a sense of self—whatever it takes to get maximum response from my muscles. This is what gives me shape, definition, density, and muscle quality. Heavy training alone may develop thicker muscles, but the resulting appearance is more like that of the powerlifter with muscular separation. The refinement is absent.

I see bodybuilding as a form of technology that has evolved to a high degree of sophistication. Perfection comes with time, work, experience, and open-mindedness. There are no shortcuts. I know from experience that it's glorious to stand on the Mr. Olympia posing platform. But I think the pursuit of perfection itself is the most ennobling experience of all.

It's War!

by Mike Mentzer

Oh, how I would howl at the titles emblazoned so boldly and unabashedly across the pages of those cherished issues of Joe Weider's magazines from the '50s, '60s, and '70s! Certainly Joe was pandering to our warlike fantasies with such gems as: "Try These New 100 Megaton Back Bombers" and "Blast Your Chest with These New Bombing Techniques."

Or so I thought at the time.

That particular trend in articles reached a high in 1975 with an article by Armand Tanny that borrowed from the headlines of the day: "In the War for Muscle There Is No Detente!"

Apparently I wasn't the only reader who found it difficult to take those articles seriously. They gradually disappeared and were replaced with tamer titles aimed at the more "serious" bodybuilder. Titles such as "What It Takes to Build Pecs Like These" and "Bodybuilding Is Lifestyle Medicine" became the new order of the day.

It's only been in the last couple of years, while training for the Mr. Universe and Mr. Olympia titles, that the significance of Joe's wordplay has dawned on me. Already a top title-winner who considered himself something of an expert on training, I realized that, in fact, the Master Blaster was not joking. He was trying to drive home an important point about training to all aspiring champions.

What General Joe Weider was attempting to do with those bellicose articles was instill in his host of readers and students an attitude that's an absolute prerequisite for reaping optimal benefits. An attitude I now call "siege mentality."

How many of you have been following an impeccable diet, training with the latest Weider Principles such as Pre-Exhaustion and Negative Reps, and are still not progressing at a satisfactory rate?

In such cases I strongly suspect that the culprit is the attitude the bodybuilder carries with him to the gym. Many come into the gym in the evening, for instance, feeling defeated, perhaps having been royally chewed out by their bosses just an hour earlier. Their workouts will most likely end up a wishy-washy affair, lacking the ferocious intensity required for optimal progress. What is required if a bodybuilder hopes to realize the most from his workouts and become a champion is an attitude befitting a hero, one full of fury. Once he enters the gym, all else is forgotten and he is transformed into a valiant warrior with girded loins, ready to do battle with the weights.

HISTORY LESSON

Although we are loathe to admit it, the human race is by nature bellicose. History books are chronicles of our conflicts since Day One. And as much as our society decries the horrors of war, few would have our nation's past military glory erased from the history books and forgotten. In ancient times, of course, men were hunters, and the most profitable and exciting way to live was to attack a neighboring tribe, kill its men, take its women, and loot its villages. Because the more aggressive people endured, humankind's bellicose instincts have survived.

The human race has evolved through struggle and combat. A life void of effort or struggle is enervating. Indeed, so much of civilized life today, while bestowing a certain amount of security, at the same time has withheld adventure.

Lacking a sufficient outlet for our biological drives and aggressive instincts, we are afflicted with depression and other nervous suffering—and no wonder! To flourish, the will needs a rallying point. At one time warfare gave individuals and societies that rallying point. But modern war is untenable. For myself and countless others, athletic training and sports competition provide a functional alternative to warfare.

Sport psychologists and social commentators have long noted the value of sports as an outlet for humankind's more aggressive—even murderous—drives. Nat Hentoff wrote in the *Atlantic Monthly* that tènnis provides an outlet for his frustrated need to express power and his murderous instincts. "Better health through murder, and the corpses can easily be replaced in tins of three," wrote Hentoff. In fact, the original purpose of sports was to toughen the individual physically and psychologically for warfare.

RELEASE FROM ANXIETY

In a previous article, I noted that during the off-season, when I'm relatively inactive, my anxiety level increases and life in general seems more problematic. As soon as I'm faced with the impending challenge of a major physique competition, however, my entire psyche undergoes a profound change. My anxiety level drops to zero and the sense of laziness and vague discontent evaporates.

Everything around me—people, things, ideas—assumes a heightened sense of meaning and purpose. Like the French philosopher Jean Paul Sartre, who said he never felt more alive than when he was fighting the Germans in World War II, I find life easiest when it's hardest, i.e., when the greatest demands and privations are required.

The psychologist William James noted: "It is sweat and effort, human nature strained to its utmost and on the rack, yet getting through alive, which inspire us."

Preparing for a contest is my moral equivalent to war.

Once contest preparation commences, the gym ceases to be a mundane menagerie of grunting humans and is transformed into a mythical battlefield where the militaristic virtues of sweat, discipline, and physical courage are applauded. The gym becomes an arena where I have the opportunity to be a hero.

The night before each workout, my brother Ray and I meet to plan our strategy for the next day's assault on immortality. Like supreme military commanders planning a massive attack, we will pore over our training journals, deciding which exercises are needed for a particular body part and which scheme of sets and reps work the best.

During this nighttime summit and the next morning before the training session, Ray and I go about deliberately cultivating an aggressive warlike attitude that will carry over into the workout.

Training for the 1980 Mr. Olympia, for example, we'd arouse our dormant warrior instincts by listening to stirring classical music or hard, driving rock. Each of us had our own pieces of literature or philosophy we'd read, and often—to get really psyched—we'd quote aloud from G. Gordon Liddy's book, *Will.* At times we would even refer to the competition itself as a battle and the competitors as our adversaries.

The point is we would deliberately cultivate this attitude to the extreme, using whatever form of mental gymnastics was required, to ensure that our workouts would be as intense as possible. By the time we'd leave for Gold's Gym to work out I could feel in myself and sense in Ray an anticipatory anxiety akin to that of a soldier about to engage the enemy.

Upon contact with our "enemy," the weights, our nervous tension would explode in a burst of energy so intense that often the other bodybuilders around us would stop training and watch. We would further incite each other to even more intense efforts with such exhortations as "Rip it out of the wall!" "Throw it through the ceiling!" and "Blitz those lats to hell!"

There were instances in which, while waiting to do my next set, I'd be shaking with rage.

In addition to being a fun and perhaps even therapeutic way of training, these workouts were, of course, intended to make the greatest possible progress. To say that our aggressive approach was successful would be an understatement. During less than a month—from July 25, 1980 to August 18, 1980—my body weight went from 207 to 214 pounds, while tests showed that I had lost 3 pounds of fat at the same time. My actual lean body mass or muscle gain was 10 pounds, while Ray's was slightly less at eight pounds. Such spectacular gains in so short a period are to be attributed as much to an inspired, aggressive training attitude as they are to training methodology.

If a beginner could sustain such an attitude and approach to his training indefinitely, he could reach the upper limits of his physical potential in two years! Most bodybuilders find it

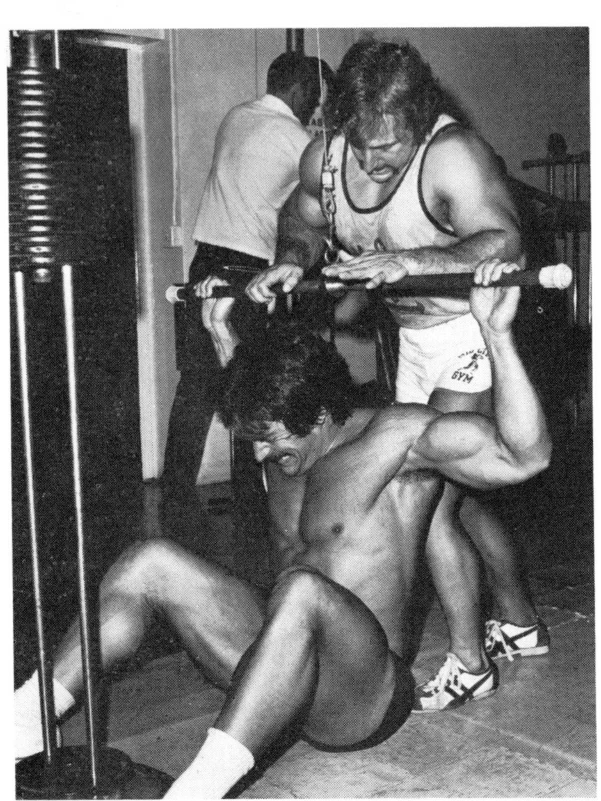

difficult to ever motivate themselves sufficiently to train as hard as is required to attain their maximum progress.

There will be others, however, who can dig deep and find the drive to train harder than they had ever before dreamed possible, to "exceed themselves," as Joe Weider advises *Muscle & Fitness* readers each month. These are the individuals who will become champions.

So keep in mind that even the most productive of the Weider Training Principles will prove fruitless if they are approached with a defeatist attitude. Undreamed-of results are just the next workout away if only you'll do as Ray and I did, and develop a more aggressive attitude toward your training. The Weiderisms "bombing and blitzing" will take on a new and greater meaning and become a part of your everyday vocabulary.

Now get to it, Weider Wildcat. Give 'em hell!

Muscle Building Without Breaks

by Boyer Coe

I don't believe in taking training layoffs. I do believe in peaking and competing several times a year. Indeed, I've competed up to 15 times each year since 1964.

Traditionally, bodybuilders are supposed to take layoffs several times a year to avoid burning out. And numerous top bodybuilders firmly believe that if they peak more than once or twice per year their bodies will be devastated by injuries.

A lot of *Muscle & Fitness* readers, as well as many of my fellow Olympians, will think I'm a maverick for saying this, but I believe that if you train properly, you *can* train year-round, and you *can* compete 6–8 times a year with a minimum of injuries. In nearly 20 years of competition, I've had only two injuries (both of them minor). That's because I cycle train.

The whole premise behind cycle training is that you alternate periods of restful, low-intensity workouts with brief periods of high-intensity precontest training. If this procedure is followed religiously, you can use your "down" cycles to build up a weak body part and actively rest your body. And during your "up" cycles you can gradually work harder and harder—as well as diet—to reach peak contest condition.

During the course of a year, there are certain shows that just automatically shift my momentum and enthusiasm into high gear for a super peak. Usually my most important contest each year is the Olympia, but after my experience in Sydney last year, I chose not to compete in the 1981 Mr. Olympia contest.

Although I bypassed the Olympia, I'm presently training very hard because the World Grand Prix Finals in Montreal are only six weeks off. I'm determined to be at my all-time best for that show. Since it was my personal decision not to compete in the Olympia, I feel I *must* defeat the Olympia winner and runners-up at Montreal.

The point I am making is that certain shows automatically guarantee me peak momentum and maximum shape. At other times I have to cooly calculate my peaks; at such times my final condition isn't quite as good—for obvious reasons.

Peaking takes its toll on any bodybuilder, both mentally and physically. Hours of training, posing practice, tanning, aerobic workouts, iso-tension contraction sessions, strict dieting, and the mental stress of competition can turn the strongest bodybuilder into a physical and emotional wreck the day after a show. And this is the time when most bodybuilders take long layoffs to mentally and physically recuperate, as well as to allow minor injuries to heal.

Physiologically, layoffs are counterproductive. You're much better off taking a period of what Soviet weightlifters call "active rest." During this time I do bodybuilding workouts of lesser intensity. I also concentrate on building up my weakest body part.

You should begin each off-season cycle with a thorough evaluation of your physique as it appeared during your last competition. Look critically at every photo of yourself that you can obtain. Ask qualified individuals, such as contest judges, for a critique of your physique. In the end, the evaluation should identify any weak points in your physique. In particular, it should isolate your weakest body part.

Let's assume that in three months you have another show coming up. Under such circumstances I'd recommend a two-month off-season cycle and a one-month peaking cycle. So where do you start?

First, resist the postcontest temptation to pig out on junk foods. I know that virtually all bodybuilders overindulge themselves as a reaction to several weeks of strict dieting. But this is a mistake. Some bodybuilders gain as much as 25–30 pounds in the weeks right after a show. Then they have to diet even more strictly for their next contest.

I keep my body weight within 6–8 pounds of contest shape at all times. This way, dieting is never the ordeal for me that it is for many other bodybuilders. And, by dieting sensibly year-round, I have more energy to keep my training poundages high (which allows me to maintain greater muscle mass) than if I had to crash diet prior to a contest.

You can relax your diet during an off-season cycle—and even eat a little of your favorite junk food occasionally. But your diet should still be healthful and nutritious. You should keep your caloric intake at a level where you can maintain a reasonably low body fat percentage. A nutritious diet should include plenty of protein, fresh vegetables, fresh fruits, natural starches (such as rice and potatoes), and vitamins and minerals each day. During this stage you can allow yourself to eat some milk products and even a little red meat now and then.

Follow a four-day training cycle at first. On the first day you should follow the Weider Muscle Priority Training Principle by training only your weakest body part. Bomb the daylights out of it with heavy weights and maximum training intensity. If you do that everytime you train that body part, it's bound to start improving.

On the next two workout days, train half your body one day and half the next. But keep these workouts playful, short, and of low intensity. All you're after here is maintenance of the stronger parts of your physique. And, of course, you are taking a period of active rest.

On the fourth day of your cycle take a complete rest from bodybuilding training. You can and should, however, engage in 30–60 minutes of some type of enjoyable aerobic activity. Take a bicycle trip with a friend, go dancing, play touch football, or a pick-up basketball game. Do any exercise, other than bodybuilding, that's enjoyable and elevates your pulse rate. This allows you to maintain a fair level of aerobic conditioning, and will make your intense precontest aerobic training seem easier.

After four weeks on a four-day cycle, begin to intensify your training a little by eliminating one rest day. This means you will string six training days together in two three-day groupings before resting on the seventh day. Keep bombing your weak body part, and gradually begin to intensify your training for the rest of your body. Follow this type of off-season cycle for four weeks.

At this point you'll be ready to begin your precontest training cycle. Divide your body into three parts, counting your previous weak point as just another body part. Then train each major muscle group twice a week, your calves 4–6 times a week, and your abdominals virtually every day. Train longer and harder every workout, and try to keep your poundages high so your muscle mass remains at a maximum. And, finally, train faster and faster, incorporating the Weider Quality Training Principle.

At this time you should also begin daily aerobic workouts (I run with my Legg Shoes, plus I ride a stationary bike 1–2 hours a day). Pose each day, and use the Weider Iso-Tension Contraction Training Principle daily for each muscle group. Cut back on your caloric intake sufficiently to reach peak muscularity. Get a good tan. And get your mind geared toward winning.

The day of your competition represents the end of your peaking cycle. Then, win or lose, evaluate the results of your complete off-season and precontest cycles, and begin the whole process over again.

Cycle after cycle, your physique will gradually improve. So get with it. Cycle training can make you a champion!

The Ghost in the Machine

by Mike Mentzer

A bodybuilder of any experience need not be told that the process of stimulating muscle growth beyond normal levels is slow indeed. It is, in fact, a harsh reality that the weight athlete is reminded of every day. And while it is patently true that some of us grow faster than others, no one grows fast enough for his or her liking.

The physiological principles that mediate the muscle growth process apply to all humans. Because the biochemical changes resulting in muscle are the same in everyone, the basic training requirements for inducing growth are also essentially the same for everyone. But if the physiology underlying muscle growth is universal and we all have practically the same training requirements, why do such dramatic differences in individual response to training exist?

GENETIC TRAITS

The citadel of bodybuilding orthodoxy rests on impressive pillars, a few of which are beginning to show cracks, revealing themselves as monumental superstitions. One of these pillars has it that anyone can reach the top if only he or she can find the right training program. Implicit in this belief is the notion that we all require different training programs and, contingent upon our ability to discover such a program, everyone has the potential to become a bodybuilding champion.

This belief has come under fire lately as a few facts derived from genetic science have cast a new light on the subject of a person's potential in bodybuilding. The mystery surrounding individual training requirements and differences in individual potential has been solved. The key is deoxyribonucleic acid, DNA, the genetic material that determines our individual inherited traits.

While the physiological principles involved in muscle are common to everyone, it is also true that there are genetic factors which modify individual response to exercise and training. Two of the most commonly recognized differences are race and sex. There are other factors, however, often less tangible, which play an even greater role in individual response to exercise.

Individuals inherit characteristics peculiar to their parents and not common to the species as a whole, e.g., facial appearance, hair color, body type, and blood type. These are "fixed" genetic traits and therefore are not subject to progressive alteration. There exist other inherited traits or tendencies, however, such as intelligence and muscle size, that are not fixed and can be altered.

The genes (hereditary material within a cell) responsible for mature body size can't find expression in an individual deprived of adequate nutrients during the early stages of growth. The same condition applies to a person's intelligence; deprived of early intellectual stimulation, the intellect will not mature. These environmental influences are necessary to develop normal levels of physical size and intelligence. To develop above-normal levels of size and intelligence, a person must expose himself or herself to demands and the performance of tasks greater than those encountered in daily living.

By following the advice mentioned above, anyone can improve upon his or her existing levels of size and intellect. In all cases, however, limits will exist and these limits are genetically predetermined. Nothing you do can extend the upper reaches of your genetic limits.

Aside from the psychological factors necessary to pursue any goal to fulfillment, there exists a constellation of genetic traits. This assemblage is the single most important consideration in building an award-winning physique. Though anyone can improve upon his or her existing level of physical development with proper training and nutrition, only those with an abundance of the required genetic traits will become champions. These traits are skeletal formation, physical proportions, somatotype, muscle fiber density, and muscle belly length.

Skeletal Formation

The most readily visible characteristic necessary in the building of a top physique is the skeletal structure. The size and formation of the individual's bones dictate how much muscle mass can be supported as well as determine the aesthetic quality of the physique. A bodybuilder with a bone structure as small and as frail as Woody Allen's could never develop—let alone support—the musculature of The Hulk. One who possesses the tanklike skeleton of a Paul Anderson could most likely develop more muscle mass than a top bodybuilding champion. But, more important, such an individual could never acquire the aesthetic flow and taper of a large billowing muscle belly into a nice tight joint, the hallmark of a bodybuilder's physique.

Physical Proportions

Superior athletes in any sport possess physical proportions ideally suited to their sport. Sprinters usually have short torsos, narrow hips, and long legs. The ideal proportions of a middle linebacker would be long torso, short legs, wide hips, and long arms. Being less performance athletes, bodybuilders require balanced proportions since their sport is more aesthetic.

Somatotype

Another generic trait plainly evident is a person's body type. Characteristics included in a discussion of body types are percentage of body fat, bone length, thigh to lower leg ratio, and lean body weight. Such characteristics will play a major role in how far an aspiring competitive bodybuilder might go. These factors should not be central to the individual's enjoyment of bodybuilding, however. Body type assessments should be used only to establish expectations of success, which will give the individual a perspective on his training.

Muscle Fiber Density

A genetic trait that's "invisible" is muscle fiber density, the number of fibers within a given volume of a muscle. One whose pectorals have one-third the number of fibers of his training partner's will still appear to have smaller pecs even if he doubles their size while his partner's remain the same (provided the former's pecs were proportionately smaller to begin with). Some believe that hyperplasia (the splitting of muscle fibers) can take place when a muscle is exposed to repeated contractions of a high-intensity nature. If hyperplasia did take place with any regularity, however, we would see advanced bodybuilders making dramatic improvements in chronically weak body parts since the increase in the number of fibers would increase the mass/density potential of a muscle. This we never see.

Length of the Muscle

While it's the size of the skeleton that enables an individual to support massive muscles with great contractile power, the ultimate size a muscle might develop is dictated primarily by its length. The length of the muscle from where its tendon attaches at one end to where its tendon attaches at the other end—that is what determines how much mass that particular muscle will have.

Examples of muscle lengths that can easily be measured are the biceps brachii, the triceps, the forearm flexors, and the gastrocnemius. If you were to take a tape to 6'5" Lou Ferrigno's biceps you would find it to measure nine inches in length, while 5'3" Danny Padilla's would measure only six inches. Since Lou's biceps are 50% longer than Danny's, they possess the capacity to develop 2.25 (1.5 × 1.5) times the cross-sectional area and 3.375 (1.5 × 1.5 × 1.5) times the volume of Danny's biceps. While Lou does have greater mass than Danny, however, that does not mean that his biceps appear more massive for his height.

The subject of muscle length is interesting when you consider randomization within an individual's musculature. A person with full-length biceps, for instance, does not necessarily possess full-length calves, or anything else for that matter. It is unusual to see a person with uniform muscle length/size over the entire body. The only person I can think of who developed extraordinary muscle mass in all his body parts is Sergio Oliva.

TRAINING REQUIREMENTS AND ULTIMATE CAPACITY

None of the genetic traits described above can be changed by training. Training can, however, enable the individual to reach the upper limits of his or her potential. Even those chosen few, the "genetic freaks," who possess a superabundance of the required traits, will improve faster and go further if they train and diet intelligently. Only by using the Weider Progressive Resistance Principle of constantly increasing training intensity can you fulfill your potential. A person of inferior genetic endowment might even surpass one of greater endowment by training properly. Since ultimate capacity to develop is a summation of genetic traits, however, it remains true that superior development will occur when superior genetic endowment is married to intelligent training.

If you have been making an honest assessment of your potential over a period of time and believe you are severely limited, don't despair. While it remains an immutable fact that genetic limitations represent a boundary over which we have no control at present (though genetic engineers may learn to manipulate it very soon) an individual's ultimate potential is something that can be assessed with any degree of accuracy only in retrospect. Therefore, don't give up your devotion to hard training and strict dieting, since

you'll never really know until you try! Frank Zane, allegedly of lesser genetic endowment, had no way of knowing what the future had in store for him when he began training. It was his unrelenting drive that allowed him to achieve so much in the sport of bodybuilding.

Unfortunately, it is true that we can't all be superstars, as nature was stingy in doling out her gifts. What is important is that each and every individual reach full potential so that he or she can enjoy a rich and rewarding life beyond merely having well-developed muscles.

Burnt Out!

by Dr. Franco Columbu

How often have we seen it happen? The bodybuilder trains hard, eats right, allows sufficient time for recuperation—yet he is burning out. He's doing all the right things, but he seems incapable of making progress.

It may not be the bodybuilder's training, diet, or recuperative ability that's at fault here. It could very well be his ability to handle his lifestyle generally. Pressures and tensions away from the gym—job, social life, marriage—can have a marked effect on a bodybuilder's progress. That's why the holistic approach to bodybuilding is vitally important for maximizing gains.

"Burning out," an expression that originated during the Industrial Revolution, described the situation when a device that went round and round became inoperative in time through excessive heat or friction.

Today "burnout" is the term used to describe a condition produced when a sport, job, or one's home life is either too stressful or monotonous. When an athlete quits, breaks down, or loses competitive drive before he or she has reached full potential, that athlete has burned out. When a worker is generally depressed and cynical, has trouble concentrating on his tasks, and snaps at his coworkers during the day and his family at night, he has burned out.

The message to the bodybuilder is: *get all of your life in order if you want to benefit most from your training.*

Of course, the way in which one gets one's life "in order" is a matter of personal choice with each bodybuilder. A championship caliber bodybuilder may decide to dedicate himself to the sport to such an extent that he quits his job (that approach, of course, can have its own set of stresses). Another individual might simply decide to switch jobs or reduce the stress in his life through relaxation therapy or improving his communication skills. As educational psychologist Dr. Claude Brodeur says, "By learning positive ways of saying things other than through punishment, threats, or sarcasm, and by watching our speech patterns, we exert control over our lives."

Whatever approach you choose, you owe it to yourself to reduce the stress in your everyday life—not only for the sake of your bodybuilding, but for the sake of your health generally. As you probably know, stress has been called "the hidden killer." It's an apt description.

The way to reduce your day-to-day stress level is to learn more about the burnout syndrome and how to recognize it. The term "burnout" doesn't identify a specific medical condition. It describes extreme reactions to continued stress. Psychologist Pamela Ennis says burnout "describes something we all experience. It involves . . . losing zest for living every day to the fullest."

A certain amount of stress is healthy. But an excess can lead to serious problems. Psychologists feel that certain personality types are more prone to burnout than others. Most prone to this condition is the overachiever/perfectionist who takes on more responsibility than he can manage because he trusts no one but himself to do the job right.

Many of the helping professions, such as medicine, law, social work, nursing, and teaching, have a high burnout rate. The underlying reason is the idealism and the expectations that motivate people to choose these fields.

The telltale signs of burnout can be seen in this self-test devised by psychoanalyst Herbert J. Freudenberger. Review your feelings during the past six months, and answer the questions with the numbers 1 through 5 to indicate the degree of change you've noticed (1 means little or none; 5 indicates a great deal).

Stress Self-Test

1. Do you tire easily?
2. Do people tell you, "You don't look so good lately"?
3. Are you working harder and accomplishing less?
4. Are you increasingly cynical and disenchanted?
5. Are you often invaded by a sadness you can't explain?
6. Are you forgetting things such as appointments and deadlines?
7. Are you increasingly irritable? Short-tempered? Disappointed in the people around you?
8. Are you seeing close friends and family members less frequently?
9. Are you too busy to do even routine things like make phone calls, read reports, or send out Christmas cards?
10. Are you suffering from aches, pains, headaches, a lingering cold?
11. Do you feel disoriented when the activity of the day comes to a halt?
12. Is joy elusive?
13. Are you unable to laugh at a joke about yourself?
14. Does sex seem more trouble than it's worth?
15. Do you have very little to say?

If your final score is 15–25, Prof. Freudenberger says you're doing fine. If it's 26–35, there are things you should be watching. If it's 36–50, you are a candidate for burning out; 51–65, you are burning out; and over 65, you're in a dangerous situation.

Burnout can occur when an individual is caught up in a game he doesn't want to play. If training for competitive bodybuilding is no longer enjoyable, it's time to give up competition, alter your training, or take a long rest.

You have to love bodybuilding to keep it up. You have to be content, your motives have to be worthy and pure, you have to be able to put up with the slow-growth periods. It's not wise to try to become an instant success. You must accept the fact that it takes years to become a great bodybuilder.

The bodybuilders who will survive are the

ones who are self-motivated, who have an internal desire to succeed. They're not in the sport to seek the praise of others (although praise is always nice). They measure their success by their own standards rather than society's.

We are heirs to the Judeo-Christian ethic which considers honest, hard work the sure road to success. For Americans, winning is often everything. We glorify the winners and look down on the losers. We see the winner as having a more exciting personality, being better looking, and having more sex appeal. We feed our own egos with winners, never losers. And we back ourselves into a corner by this type of thinking in our own athletic, occupational, or personal endeavors. Woe be it to us if we slide from grace by losing.

The unrelieved pace and pressure of living today has caused more cases of burnout than ever before. In every endeavor where a person is forced to deal with intensifying demands, there are serious reactions.

Burnout can come from the pressures of school work, the demands of a job, or the emotional involvement of a love affair. Such stressful situations can drain the energy needed for bodybuilding training and make full recuperation almost impossible.

It's important not to let these stresses drain the energy needed for your workouts. Repeated, frustrated attempts to train with lowered energy establishes a pattern of failure that can lead directly to burnout.

An individual must have control of his life and must develop a positive lifestyle without the insidious energy drain of depressing thoughts and resultant failure.

Bodybuilding is holistic. When you have full control over the mental, physical, and emotional affairs of your life, then you will realize the best and most enduring results of your bodybuilding training. Once you master your life, it will pay off in everything you do—in the gym and out.

Is There a Magic Formula?

by Rick Wayne

It's an interesting, if lamentable, irony of our time that the most educated among us, that is to say, the most informed, often appear to be the most confused. An extraterrestrial visitor might quickly deduce from our behavior that ours is indeed a nation of shopkeepers. It seems that everyone has built that better mousetrap and is hell-bent on attracting the world to his door. We rise each day with one thought: how best to hawk mediocrity.

At every turn we are bombarded by television and newspaper entreatments to buy the latest "clinically-tested" soap powder, advertisements that too often turn out to be sugar-coated invitations to do ourselves in, physically or mentally. Browbeaten by the hard sell, we are fast becoming incapable of discerning the con from the contrary. We determine a man's worth not by the proven quality of his work but by his ability to turn it into a buck. We voluntarily sacrifice our health for the empty promises of some untested wonder pill. We gladly accept thalidomide as the cure for insomnia, then pay with a lifetime of misery. The sugar bowl has replaced the fruit bowl on our table, and we casually sacrifice our natural environment on the radioactive cross of progress. Small wonder that for many of us the American Dream is fast becoming synonymous with LSD trips.

We are a confused lot. Even our leading muscle magazines are not above reproach. Recently, this tidbit was offered as food for thought to ambitious bodybuilders: "Lifting twice weekly, using a given number of sets per muscle group, is just as effective as lifting three times a week employing the same number of sets and reps."

The writer then went on to state that "the magic number of training days per week for optimal strength development has not been firmly established because each individual is unique. The number of days you should train will be determined not only by your recuperative powers, mental attitude, rate of progression . . . but also by whether strength is your prime goal."

Implicit here is the suggestion that the reader discard everything the writer offered in two previous pages of advice and determine for himself the training schedule best suited to his particular characteristics. Much ado about nothing. Years ago, Joe Weider said it so much simpler in his published dissertation, *The Instinctive Training Principle*.

Franco Columbu, the current Mr. Olympia, supports Joe. "We hear so much these days about the so-called science of bodybuilding," says Franco, "and if we're not careful we could

Rod Koontz.

end up confused and frustrated. I like things that are basic, uncomplicated. The boxer who is too concerned with the science of boxing soon develops a deaf ear to his natural instincts. And soon he'll be easy meat in the ring. It's the same with bodybuilding. A young man shouldn't take up the sport because he thinks he can make a career out of it. He'll need at least two years before he can know whether he has what it takes to be Mr. America."

As Franco tells it, the beginner should follow a basic training schedule that comprises Bench Presses, Squats, Rows, Lateral Raises, Curls, and Chins.

"Such a training routine will help the beginner develop the body's big muscles and, with that, strength," he says. "Instead of concerning himself with the theories, the pseudosciences, the magic reps-sets formulas, the beginner should concentrate on developing power and size. To do so he must eat naturally and train naturally."

Naturally? Yes, says Franco, it's the only way to go. The beginner should strive to increase his training poundages, but only as his natural abilities allow him.

"For example, it might take a full month before a beginner can increase his Bench Press by 10 pounds," says the two-time Mr. Olympia. "The fact that Mike Mentzer or Boyer Coe is able to bench 400 pounds for 10 reps should in no way dictate the pace of the beginner's workout. Mike and Boyer might offer fantastic inspiration, but the beginner should always remember that the two champions started out with a heap of natural talent, talent the beginner may not have."

So while the beginner should push himself in his efforts at improvement, he should do so with care. Championship bodies are not created overnight, says Franco.

"There is another factor that too many bodybuilders ignore," he adds. "And that is health. If your body isn't healthy, if you do not eat sensibly, the time spent at the gym will not be as productive as it might have been."

A basic bodybuilding diet, where Franco is concerned, comprises "lots of eggs, fish, and meat. And fresh vegetables." He says many bodybuilders ignore potatoes and stuff themselves with salads in the erroneous belief that they'll build muscle that way, when salads are primarily water.

"My experiences and my studies tell me clearly that restrictive diets are hell on bodybuilding," says Franco. "They interfere with training, leave you weak before workout sessions, and weaker still afterwards. As a result recuperation is slow."

All the bodybuilder needs to know is this: protein builds muscle, and carbohydrates supply the energy required for productive training.

"A good idea might be to eat a substantial carbohydrate meal before each workout," says Franco. "Give yourself at least one hour between your last meal and your workout. Never stuff yourself. Never train on a full stomach. Fish, potatoes, fruit—these will give you all the energy you require."

Bodybuilders who stick to the erroneous belief that protein alone benefits bodybuilding soon discover that they cannot train as hard as they wish. The spirit might be willing, Franco points out, but the muscle is often too weak to oblige. And the bodybuilders' energy levels are always lower than their expectations.

When it comes to reps and sets, there is no magic formula, by Franco's account. Each muscle group requires a different approach. Basically, some body parts do best on a system of 8–10 reps. Others seem to benefit best from sets of 10–15.

"From my own efforts, and from watching the results achieved by others with whom I've trained over the years, it seems the best way to gain density and muscle power is to train heavy," says Franco. "By that I mean, you should bench press with a weight that will allow a minimum of six reps without too much difficulty, but demands assistance from a training partner if you want to force out 10."

In other words, the beginner shouldn't bench press with weights that hardly work up a sweat. He should look upon the exercise as a power-builder, a movement that can help him develop upper body mass, particularly in the pecs and shoulders. But for best results he should keep his reps no lower than six and no higher than 10.

Franco points out that it's folly to attempt heavy poundages until the body has been prepared for such stress.

"Always warm up," he says. "Do your first set of Bench Presses with a weight that will comfortably allow 10 repetitions. Then start packing on the plates."

When it comes to movements such as Dumbbell Flyes and Parallel Bar Dipping, Franco recommends 10–15 repetitions, "and quick sets."

He takes his time with the heavy movements, as much time as his instinct dictates—which is not to say he fools around between sets. As he says, he goes to the gym for one purpose only, and that's not to bullshoot with friends! With the high-rep movements, however, Franco is like a high-balling freight.

"I should point out that the actual performance of each rep should be deliberate," he says. "Each rep must be done with intense concentration. I try to think cuts into my pecs or deltoids or whatever muscle group I'm training."

How many sets?

"Again that depends on the muscle group," Franco says. "I've found that 12 sets work best for the small areas, such as the biceps and triceps, the deltoids, and so on. My calves are something else. Here I depend on what I call shock treatment. Some days I'll do heavy weights and high sets, up to 20 sets, then at other times I might do 15 sets or less with greater concentration and speed. Anything to keep those devils off-guard."

In the last analysis, however, Franco advises the bodybuilder to trust his own body. The articles that appear in the bodybuilding mags should never be taken as Holy Writ. They should serve only to guide and inspire. Franco points out that Fox, Mentzer, Robinson, and the other champions have all discovered little secrets over the years. But such secrets are never guaranteed to yield satisfactory results for every weight athlete.

"The smart bodybuilders will try out the different methods advocated with great care," says Franco, "and he will take notes on the way they affect him. Then finally he must decide for himself what system of sets and reps work best for him, which foods serve him best, and so on. Above all, he should always consider his health before any promised muscle gains."

Mike Mentzer's detractors like to point out, "if his system were any good, he would have wiped out Frank Zane and the other top guys. And he hasn't."

Of course, that's one load of road apples. For the value of a training system may not necessarily be synonymous with the results of contests as determined by human judges.

The truth is that in a very short time Mentzer rose from the rank and file to place an extremely close second to Frank Zane in the 1979 Olympia. By now the subsequent Olympia requires no further comment from me.

Of course, the intrepid Mentzer sometimes invites egg in the face. Hear him: "It is my contention that bodybuilding, as it is currently practiced in many places, is the most counterproductive, least scientific endeavor that anyone could possibly engage in."

He casts a cold eye upon the so-called bodybuilding authorities. "All the muscle magazines purport to be scientific journals, so show me the scientists on their editorial staff. Who conducts the scientific investigations alluded to each month? Casual observation of misguided bodybuilders in a gym can hardly be regarded as scientific research."

Is Mentzer suggesting that bodybuilders should investigate for themselves? Hardly. "How many bodybuilders have the capacity for serious scientific investigation? How many know the least thing about scientific investigation?"

Mentzer is not swayed by the results achieved by such established champions as Padilla or Robinson. "It all goes to prove how much more these people might have achieved with scientific training procedures," Mike counters.

The key to building big muscles, he says, is training intensity, by which he means that the harder a man trains, the less amount of training he'll be able to do. Confusing? Let Mike illustrate:

"It's like the distance runner and the sprinter. The sprinter always has larger calves even though he actually engages in only a small fraction of the amount of work done by the distance runner."

The distance runner, he points out, has long, lean muscle while the sprinter has more muscular mass.

Mentzer does not buy the idea that some body parts require more sets and reps than others. Muscles respond in the same way to the same stimulus, he says. There is no man who can sprint at top speed for a mile. "He's running too hard, too *intensely* to last a mile. The harder you engage in a physical activity, which is to say, the more intensely you push yourself, the less of it you'll be able to withstand."

Which is why Mike believes that bodybuilders who say they do 20 sets a body part and claim to train three hours a day, six days a week "are not training hard."

He likens his own training to that of a sprinter. Both work fast, and as heavy as possible.

"While it's true that I'm not running," says Mentzer, "I nevertheless move weights as fast as I can go. The intensity of my training is actually greater than the sprinter's since I can adjust the amount of weight used. The sprinter moves only his body weight. I increase my training poundage, the training intensity, at will."

He points out that intensity is a function of power input. You move weight distances in a certain amount of time. "So if you can increase the weight, increase the distance, and decrease the speed, well then you'll be increasing your power input geometrically."

Whereas many bodybuilders do from 12–20 sets of exercises for the upper arms, Mentzer usually does no more than four. He allows that he does a bit more for his back, maybe six or seven sets, "because there are so many different areas to be worked: the lats, the teres, lower back, traps, and so on."

By Mike's account, he is able to gain weight and muscle mass very quickly only because he does not burn himself out. "I never appear worn out at contests, and I'm always strong, contrary to other bodybuilders who appear emaciated onstage and are always talking about how they had to dry out for cuts. The correct way to get into contest condition is to build the muscles to their full potential, then diet to bring out the cuts and striations."

Consider the way Mike trains his biceps: "After warming up with Chins or whatever exercise I might fancy on a given day, I go straight into Curls on the preacher bench with 150 pounds on a cambered bar. I do four rapid reps, with emphasis on the slow, downward pull. By the time I've done the first set my biceps have had it. That one set would have been sufficient, but I do another. In the end, my biceps feel totally wasted. Twenty sets would have been counterproductive. Those extra 18 would have done nothing to stimulate muscle growth. All they'd have done was to tear down my energy and recuperative capacity, precisely what I try to avoid in the interest of muscle growth.

"Bodybuilders don't realize that the first concern of the body is to acquire and reserve energy," Mike goes on. "The first thing your body does after a workout is to try to recover the energy used up in training. If there is some left after your workout, hell, you won't be able to stop yourself from growing!"

On the other hand, Franco maintains that the little muscles, e.g., the posterior deltoids, the outer head of the biceps, the serratus, inter alia, require special treatment. He contends that slow concentration Curls have a shaping effect on the biceps, for example, that cannot be achieved from heavy preacher Curls. And he claims that while Mike's methods might develop power and muscle mass—which serve well in weightlifting and powerlifting contests—they won't produce the kind of physique for which, say, Zane is famous.

The controversy promises to be with us for a long time. One thing for certain, however: the ground rules remain constant. The beginner should be careful not to overextend himself. He should not allow his ambitions to overwhelm logic. He must give himself latitude. He must allow the training routines he follows sufficient time to do their stuff.

Above all, the beginner should not attempt the poundages, nor the stressful workouts, outlined by the champions. Even in this prefab age, Rome could not be built in a day. The magazines you read may offer inspiration, but let good sense guide you. Be discerning; try to separate what is obviously a sales gimmick from fact.

Joe Weider on Running

by Joe Weider

Used correctly, distance running is the best form of aerobic exercise. I enjoy and benefit from running 30 minutes three or four times per week. But I'm deeply concerned that the current running revolution is running millions of healthy men and women into the ground.

To achieve optimum health and physical fitness you must do three types of training—weight training (for strength and well-toned muscular development), stretching, and aerobic workouts. These three types of exercise are like the legs of a tripod supporting a heavy brick of gold called physical fitness. If one leg of the tripod is weakened or removed, physical fitness will topple into the mud, perhaps to be lost forever.

In *Muscle & Fitness* we have always stressed the techniques and benefits of weight training and bodybuilding. In fact, since 1936, I have been championing the values of weight training. In the next section of this book, we will provide a detailed and valuable article by Bill Reynolds on the techniques and benefits of stretching. This article will provide you with the second leg of your physical fitness tripod.

Since running has become America's favorite aerobic activity we have decided to present you with the third leg of your physical fitness tripod.

Tom Platz on the run.

Here I will discuss the safe and sane way to achieve aerobic conditioning through running. By using my sensible guidelines, you'll be able to avoid the pitfalls that waylay so many runners.

RUNNING TO EXTREMES

Since Frank Shorter won the 1972 Olympic marathon (the marathon distance is 26 miles, 385 yards), there's been a boom in marathon running in America. Newsstand racks are jammed with running magazines, and more than 100 marathons are conducted each year in the United States. In the 1981 New York Marathon there were more than 10,000 participants.

This love affair with running 26.2 miles has seduced millions of men and women into taking daily (and sometimes even twice-daily) runs of 6–10 miles. Running to such extremes—particularly for the person with limited background in the sport—doesn't allow the body enough time to recover adequately between training sessions. The resulting fatigue leads to overuse injuries.

Thousands of times per day—day after day—every runner subjects his or her feet, ankles, leg muscles, knees, hips, and lower back to relentless pounding. As a result, most serious runners train with at least one minor, but persistent, joint or muscle injury. And an injury which may seem minor today can have major repercussions when you reach your 50s, 60s, and 70s.

At the start of a marathon you'll notice that the runners usually aren't discussing their competitive times, their training methods for the race, or even the weather. Instead they all seem to be discussing their *injuries*. "Yeah," says one, "I've had a lot of chondromalacia lately, but I've kept running."

Runners who train to extremes suffer from a bewildering array of injuries. Here are the most common injuries (almost all of them are related to what physicians call "overuse syndrome"):

- Achilles tendinitis or rupture
- Shin splints
- Heel bone damage
- Bursitis (usually under the kneecap, in the hips, in the toes, or between the Achilles tendon and the heel bone)
- Stress fractures
- Knee chondromalacia
- Strained or torn muscles
- Spinal compression (and related sciatica)
- Leg muscle pulls and tears
- Muscle cramps
- Blood in the urine
- Chronic dehydration
- Sprained ankles, knees, hips
- Inflamed ligaments
- Foot arch problems
- A chronically overtrained state (and related colds, flu, etc.)

Runner's World magazine surveyed its readers and found that the most common overuse injuries runners suffer affect the knees (18%), Achilles tendons (14%), shins (usually shin splints)(11%), foot arches (7%), and ankles (6%). Virtually all runners who train to extremes suffer from such injuries.

Tragically, many runners prefer to ignore pain—nature's warning that they are injured. They try to "run through" an injury, often making that injury much more serious than it would have been had they rested. One runner of our acquaintance—a man who is a veteran long-distance runner—began to notice mild sciatica pain in his hip. By attempting to run through the injury, he further compressed his spinal vertebrae, ending up flat on his back in excruciating pain for several days, and spent hundreds of dollars on chiropractic treatment. Clearly, no one should ever try to run through any running-related overuse injury.

RUNNING ISN'T ENOUGH

Another persistent habit among runners is to insist that running is the perfect form of exercise. It is true that running, done correctly, is a superior means of developing cardiorespiratory (heart-lung) fitness. However, running actually decreases body flexibility, builds little or no strength, and it doesn't develop a well-toned, muscular body. To attain all of these qualities, you must be on a regular exercise program that includes all three legs of the physical fitness tripod—weight training, stretching, and aerobic conditioning.

ALTERNATIVES TO RUNNING

Most serious runners prefer to ignore the fact that there are many other forms of physical activity that produce superior cardiorespiratory fitness.

Exercise physiologists determine the aerobic effectiveness of a type of exercise by measuring an athlete's ability to consume and efficiently process oxygen. To do this, they use what is called an "oxygen uptake test."

In terms of oxygen uptake, champion cross-country skiers consistently score higher than champion long-distance runners. And there are many other types of aerobic activity that are also very effective—and produce far fewer injuries. These activities include cycling, swimming, circuit weight training, and rowing.

THE BENEFITS OF RUNNING

So far, I suppose I've painted a rather bleak picture of running. However, as I've said, done correctly, running does have far-reaching benefits. And running, unlike cross-country skiing, rowing, or cycling, does not require special equipment, weather, or facilities. Therefore, running is certainly a more convenient method to achieve a superior level of aerobic conditioning.

Obviously, running is an excellent way to achieve optimum aerobic fitness. It strengthens the heart and circulatory system, helping to prevent cardiac disease, arteriosclerosis, strokes, and a host of other heart, lung, and circulatory diseases (a good indication of this is the lowered pulse rate runners achieve; a low pulse rate indicates superior heart and circulatory efficiency).

Running melts away excess body fat and dramatically lowers blood cholesterol and triglyceride levels. In short, if done correctly, running can make profound—and often life-prolonging—changes in the body. Therefore, I think that everyone should give running a fair trial as an aerobic conditioning method.

Ray Mentzer streaks across the beach.

A SAFE AND SANE APPROACH TO RUNNING

Based upon my own extensive experience with running, coupled with many years of research, I have developed the following 11 rules that will guide you to safe and sane running:

1. *Always combine running with weight training and stretching.* As I've mentioned, running falls far short of being the perfect form of exercise. Always be conscious of your physical fitness tripod. Don't let it topple by cutting away one of the legs.

2. *Never run two days in a row.* The reason why runners develop overuse injuries in the first place is that they run nearly every day and don't allow themselves time to recover. Dr. Kenneth

Cooper, the father of aerobics, believes that running three miles a day three days per week will give most men and women adequate aerobic fitness. I agree with him. If you feel that you need more aerobic training, try cycling or swimming on the days you aren't running.

3. *Buy good-quality running shoes.* Running shoes that cushion and support the feet cost $30–$50 per pair, and they're worth every penny. Top-quality running shoes are specifically engineered to prevent running injuries, and they do a good job of it. Running in cheap sneakers is inviting trouble.

4. *Never try to run through an injury.* If you experience pain while running, switch to swimming or cycling until your discomfort abates. Then return to running.

5. *Don't run on an uneven surface.* As long as you wear high-quality running shoes, it's often better to run on concrete than on grass. Grass surfaces can be uneven, and every ground depression you step into increases the stress on your legs. Also be careful not to run on the slanted shoulder of a road, since this puts enormous strain on your legs and lower back. And don't do too much running up and down hills.

6. *Run within your capabilities.* Never overextend yourself, either in the speed or the duration of a run. To keep from doing this, run according to time, not distance. For example, run for 20 minutes, not two miles. Timing yourself over a certain distance automatically causes you to push yourself, because you naturally want to beat your record for the distance. It's best to run easily and fluidly until you're comfortably fatigued, then stop.

7. *Progress slowly.* In the next section of this article, I'll suggest some running programs. Progress slowly and easily with them, and don't overextend yourself. When running, you needn't induce great pain or fatigue to achieve aerobic conditioning.

8. *Run in a relaxed manner to minimize jarring.* Running will be more enjoyable and less stressful if you relax during your workouts. If you feel tension in any part of your body, especially your thighs, chest, neck, or shoulders, slow to a more comfortable pace.

Many people believe that jogging is harmful but running is not, so they try to run faster than is good for them. In fact, jogging is just slow, rhythmical, relaxed running. A jogging pace is an excellent way to start out your running program. Then as your conditioning improves, you may want to increase your speed.

9. *Dress for the weather.* If you dress appropriately, you can run in very cold weather. And if you consume sufficient liquids (particularly electrolyte replacement drinks), you can run in hot weather with no ill effects. The secret is to dress for the weather. Wear a minimum of clothing when it's hot, and sufficient clothing when it's cold. In cold weather, several thin layers of clothing provide much better insulation than one or two thick layers.

10. *Make running an enjoyable habit.* Like weight training or any other form of exercise, running is more beneficial when it's done regularly. So make running a habit—a pleasant habit. If you don't enjoy it, don't run. Exercise should be something you look forward to doing each day.

11. *Forget about racing.* Racing is one of the most destructive things you can do as a runner. The thought of competition immediately causes everyone to train to excess, which leads to overuse injuries. Run for the pleasure of running and for the aerobic fitness it provides, not for a T-shirt with the name of some obscure race printed on it.

YOUR RUNNING PROGRAM

If you've been physically inactive for a long period, walk before you run. Spend two or three weeks walking every other day—going a little farther or a little faster each session. Then mix walking with short stretches of jogging. Gradually you'll condition your body until you can run steadily, albeit slowly, for 15 consecutive minutes. Then you'll be ready for a regular running program.

I run every other day, which means I am on the road three days one week and four the next. For most health- and fitness-conscious men and women, however, it's easier to run only three days per week, alternating days of running with days of weight training. You should do a stretching workout every day.

I don't think you need to run more than 30–40 minutes at a time to reach optimum aerobic conditioning. In order to work up to this level, use a gradual progression. Here is a sample program. Remember to run within your limits. If aerobic conditioning is new to you, be sure you do a lot of walking before you start a running program.

	Week One
Tuesday	15 minutes
Thursday	20 minutes
Saturday	15 minutes
	Weekly Total = 50 minutes
	Week Two
Tuesday	20 minutes
Thursday	15 minutes
Saturday	20 minutes
	Weekly Total = 55 minutes
	Week Three
Tuesday	15 minutes
Thursday	25 minutes
Saturday	20 minutes
	Weekly Total = 60 minutes
	Week Four
Tuesday	20 minutes
Thursday	25 minutes
Saturday	20 minutes
	Weekly Total = 65 minutes
	Week Five
Tuesday	25 minutes
Thursday	20 minutes
Saturday	25 minutes
	Weekly Total = 70 minutes

Try to progress slowly and gradually, staying well within your limits of strength and endurance. And don't be a slave to the schedule I've just outlined. Use it only as a guide.

RUNNING AND BODYBUILDING

Running and serious bodybuilding are very compatible. By including regular running and stretching in your bodybuilding program, you will ultimately build a better body. You'll have greater endurance for your workouts, and your body fat level will remain lower throughout the year. Running or some other type of aerobic activity will make it easier for you to cut up for competition. So I heartily recommend a running program for bodybuilders—as long as the guidelines for sensible running are followed. In fact, I'd recommend a safe and sane running program to anyone!

TRAINING ROUTINES

Stretching Exercises for Fitness

by Bill Reynolds

Bodybuilders who jog and work out with weights but still appear klutzy should take a tip from cats—the domestic as well as the jungle variety—and s-t-r-e-t-c-h.

WHY STRETCH?

There are six basic reasons why everyone should do regular stretching workouts.

1. *Stretching improves appearance.* It lengthens the muscles, giving you the long, lean, sensuous, well-toned look so in vogue today.
2. *Stretching improves health and fitness.* In concert with weight training and aerobic workouts—running, cycling, swimming, rowing, etc.—stretching gives you the ultimate in health and physical fitness.
3. *Stretching prevents injuries.* Most everyday injuries and athletic injuries are caused either by trauma (a fall, a car crash, a 250-pound football player colliding with you) or by overextension of a joint, muscle, or connective tissue (muscle pulls, sprains, strains). Athletes who follow regular and progressive stretching programs suffer at least 50% fewer overextension injuries than those who don't.
4. *Stretching is a good warm-up/warm-down in conjunction with other types of training sessions.* But above and beyond this, a pre-workout stretching program improves neuromuscular coordination. And after a workout, stretching will prevent soreness, as well as promote faster physiological recovery.
5. *Stretching improves athletic performance.* A more flexible athlete will perform better. Can you, for example, conceive of a gymnast with tight muscles? Any athlete who's more flexible than another automatically has a psychological and physiological edge.
6. *Done correctly, stretching is fun.* Have you ever awakened in the morning and, still in bed, slowly stretched your entire body? It felt great, didn't it? Well, that same superbly sensual feeling can be yours every day.

WHO SHOULD STRETCH?

Every man and woman can benefit enormously from following a regular and progressive program of stretching exercises. And there are no age limits. Senior citizens can stretch often when orthopedic problems prevent them from doing other forms of exercise. Even toddlers can stretch along with Mom and Dad.

Obviously, all athletes should include stretching in their conditioning programs. Many

Standing Hamstring Stretch (start and finish above) and variations (above left and left).

professional teams now employ a flexibility coach. Paul Uram, flexibility coach of the Pittsburgh Steelers, has written *The Complete Stretching Book* (Mountain View, CA, Anderson-World, Inc., 1980, $4.95). Another excellent book is Bob Anderson's *Stretching* (Bolinas, CA, Shelter Publications, 1980, $7.95).

Some individuals are more adept at stretching than others. Generally speaking, women will be more flexible than men, and children will be far more flexible than adults.

WHY BODYBUILDERS SHOULD STRETCH

During the past couple of years, several bodybuilders—most notably World Cup winner, Boyer Coe—have discovered that stretching is an excellent supplement to bodybuilding training.

"It builds bigger, better-quality muscles," Boyer recently told me. "The first time I seriously used stretching workouts was before the last Olympia. Everyone there said I had improved 25%–30% since the previous Mr. O. I'm convinced that stretching is a superior adjunct to bodybuilding training."

WHEN TO STRETCH

Having been a flexibility, strength, and endurance coach to hundreds of pro and amateur athletes, I have come to some very definite conclusions about stretching. First, anyone who is serious about improving his/her flexibility, health, appearance, and athletic performance should stretch every day for at least 10–15 minutes. Stretching 3–4 times per week will slowly improve joint and muscle flexibility, but daily stretching will increase flexibility 4–5 times more quickly. And I've gotten tremendous results with some very inflexible athletes by putting them on a twice-a-day stretching program.

If you participate in some other form of exercise, the best time to stretch is as a warm-up for that activity. Many men and women do this subconsciously. You've no doubt seen a runner briefly stretch his/her calves before setting out for a run, or a basketball player quickly stretch his/her hamstrings before going into a game. Such an abbreviated stretching session does very little for the athlete, however.

To be effective as a warm-up, such a stretching session should last 10–15 minutes and include flexibility exercises for every part of the body. Done in this same manner, a stretching workout also acts as an excellent warm-down following a game or workout. You'll be truly amazed at how quickly you can recuperate if you do 10–15 minutes of stretching after exercise.

For the average person, it's best to stretch in the evening—perhaps while watching television—an hour or two before bedtime. This will relieve all the tensions you've built up during the day and give you a "stretcher's high" akin to a "runner's high" or the "pump" a bodybuilder experiences. After an evening stretching workout, you'll be relaxed and will sleep peacefully.

HOW TO STRETCH

I'm totally amazed at the abusive ways some men and women do their stretching exercises. They stretch too hard or they bounce into a stretch, losing much of the value of the exercise in the process. Correctly applied, stretching is a *gentle* exercise, and unless you pursue it gently you will lose most of the benefits it can give you.

Because it's easy to injure yourself by overextending the range of motion of a joint or muscle, nature has provided your body with two protective mechanisms. Both are specialized types of neurons (nerve endings). One type senses when a muscle is being overstretched and signals this fact by feeding pain signals back to the brain.

The second type of neurons is part of a protective mechanism called the "stretch reflex." When a stretch is sensed by the second type of neurons to be progressing too quickly, the mind reflexively begins to contract the stretched muscle. And this acts as a shock absorber, slowing and then halting the stretch before the muscle can be injured. This is somewhat like the way your thigh muscles flex to absorb the shock of landing when you jump off a table onto the floor.

When you stretch a muscle group ballistically (that is, in a bouncing manner), the stretch reflex is activated and the muscle shortens to stop the stretch. So while it may seem logical to some that bouncing would intensify a stretch and bring faster results, such ballistic stretching actually has the opposite effect. Because of the stretch reflex, the stretched muscles actually shorten and you come up far short of reaching a fully stretched position.

To fully stretch a muscle (or joint), you must *slowly ease into the stretch,* in order to circumvent the stretch reflex. Take 30–40 sec-

Hamstring Stretch, Partner.

onds to move slowly into a stretch to the point where you just begin to feel slight pain in the stretched muscle. This is the maximum point to which you should stretch. I like to call this the "pain edge." And if you stretch much past this point, you can actually begin to pull tiny muscle fibers apart, injuring the muscles.

So now you have enough physiological information to understand my description of the perfect stretch. Regardless of the flexibility movement you use, take 30–40 seconds to ease into the stretch. Then once you encounter the pain edge, back off until the pain has just disappeared. Once you've reached this "stretching zone," hold the stretch in that position for 20–30 seconds (work up eventually to one or two minutes in this position). Breathe shallowly, although with normal rhythm, when holding a stretched position. Finally, relax the stretch and either repeat it a minute later or move on to another stretching movement.

If you are to receive the maximum benefit from this exercise, you must discover your personal stretching zone. It's only while holding a flexibility movement in this zone that you will derive the greatest benefit from a program of stretching.

STRETCHING PROGRESSION

Anyone who has never undertaken a stretching program—even if that person has

Hurdler's Stretch.

Hurdler's Stretch variations.

been physically active—should begin very slowly on the program outlined in this article. You can actually injure your muscles and become very sore if you push too hard. Proper stretching is virtually effortless, and yet you will slowly gain flexibility from even the easiest program.

Beginners should back away from the pain edge in their first stretching efforts and hold each stretch for only 20 seconds. They should also do only one repetition of an exercise for each muscle group. From this point, *slowly* add to the duration of each stretch (until you can hold it for a full minute) and the severity of each stretch (until you have it held in the upper range of the stretching zone, just microns from the pain edge).

Once you reach this point, you can either add repetitions to a stretch (begin a second rep by holding it for only 20 seconds, then gradually work it up to 60) or add another stretching movement for the same body part (again, begin it with a duration of only 20 seconds). For our purposes, however, I recommend doing a one-minute stretch in one exercise for each body part, a workout you'll be able to complete in 10–15 minutes.

YOUR STRETCHING EXERCISES

The stretching exercises that Shelley Gruwell, Ms. California, and Dennis Tinerino, Mr. America, have posed for here are all excellent. By comparing the photographs with the following exercise descriptions, you'll be able to easily learn every movement.

Hamstring Stretch

Emphasis—These three movements stretch the hamstring muscles at the back of your thighs.

Starting Position—In the basic Hamstring Stretch, lock your legs and extend your arms overhead, clasping your hands.

Stretched Position—Keeping your legs straight, bend over and touch your hands to your feet. As you become more and more advanced, you will actually be able to lay your torso against your thighs in this position.

Variations—Two variations of this exercise exist. In the first, the legs are spread and you bend over to grasp your legs individually with your arms (see photo). In the second, you bend slightly to the side and grasp the ankle of one leg with both hands, gently pulling your torso downward.

Hamstring Stretch, Partner

Emphasis—Again, this movement stretches the hamstring muscles.

Starting Position—With both legs held straight, stand on one foot and extend the other foot to be held by a partner (as shown) or to rest on the top of a table or other fairly high, flat surface. Your torso should be relatively upright and your arms extended forward.

Stretched Position—Bend slowly forward and try to rest your torso on your thigh. Both legs should remain fully straight throughout the movement.

Hurdler's Stretch

Emphasis—This exercise stretches both the hamstring and the groin muscles.

Starting Position—Sit on the floor (or the beach or lawn). Extend your right leg forward and lock it straight throughout the movement. Your left leg should be bent at a 90-degree angle and lying flat on the floor behind your body. Your torso should be upright and your arms extended directly forward parallel to the floor.

Stretched Position—Bend slowly forward over your right leg and grasp your ankle to gently pull your torso down to rest along your thigh. After stretching with your right leg forward, do an equal amount of stretching with your left leg extended forward.

Variation—As depicted, this stretching exercise can also be done with one leg extended directly

Seated Groin Stretch.

Standing Hip Stretch.

Lunging Stretch.

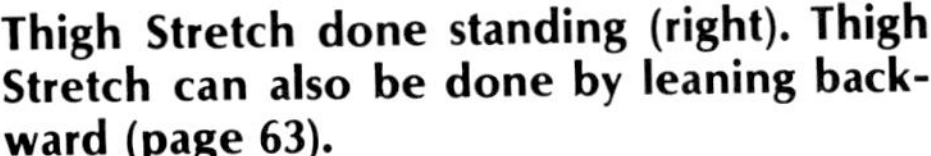

Thigh Stretch done standing (right). Thigh Stretch can also be done by leaning backward (page 63).

forward and the other held straight and extended to the side at a 90-degree angle.

Seated Groin Stretch

Emphasis—This movement stretches all the muscles of the groin and inner thighs.

Starting Position—Sit down and bend your legs as completely as possible (ideally, your heels should be right up against your pelvic structure), and position your knees close together. Grasp your knees with your hands. Be sure to keep your torso erect throughout the movement.

Stretched Position—Use your hands to slowly push your knees apart until they are as close to the floor as possible.

Standing Hip Stretch

Emphasis—This exercise stretches the hip and buttock muscles.

Starting Position—Stand erect. Balancing on your right foot and with your right leg held straight throughout the movement, bend your left leg and raise your knee up until you can grasp it with your hands.

Stretched Position—Pull up on your knee gently until you have reached the maximum range of motion for your hip and buttock muscles. Do an equal amount of stretching for both legs.

Lunging Stretch

Emphasis—This movement stretches the muscles of the hips, buttocks, and front thighs.

Starting Position—Stand erect, hands on hips.

Stretched Position—As illustrated, step forward with either leg and bend it fully while keeping the other leg fairly straight. Hold this position for the required length of time and then repeat the movement for the other leg.

Variation—Lunging stretches can also be done stepping to the side instead of directly forward, in which case, the inner thigh muscles are stressed much more directly.

Thigh Stretch

Emphasis—This exercise strongly stretches the quadriceps muscles on the front of your thighs.

Starting Position—Stand erect and balance on your left foot with your left leg held straight. Reach behind you and grasp your right ankle with your right hand, as illustrated.

Stretched Position—Pull gently upward on your ankle to stretch your thigh muscles.

Variation—As illustrated, this movement can also be done kneeling, leaning backward, and bracing your upper body with your arms. In this variation you can increase the intensity of the stretch merely by bending your arms a little. Be careful not to overdo it.

Calf Stretch.

Chest/Shoulder Stretch.

Calf Stretch

Emphasis—This exercise stretches and tones all of the muscles at the back of your lower legs.

Starting Position—Face a partner (as shown) or a wall and place your hands on the partner's shoulders or against the wall at shoulder height. Move your feet backward until your right leg, torso, and arms make a straight line. Your left leg should be bent.

Stretched Position—Gently press your heel down to the floor (or beach, as the case may be). If you can comfortably place your heel flat, put your foot back another 4–6 inches to intensify the stretch. Be sure to do an equal amount of stretching for each calf.

Chest/Shoulder Stretch

Emphasis—This movement strongly stretches the pectoral and deltoid muscles.

Starting Position—Sit down and bend your legs slightly. With your arms held straight throughout the movement, lean backward and place them on the floor (or bench).

Stretched Position—Slowly move your hands more and more to the rear, to gently stretch the chest and shoulder muscles.

Full Back, Partner Stretch

Emphasis—This exercise stretches all the muscles of the back.

Starting Position—Sit down and face your partner. With your feet about 12 inches apart, place your soles against those of your partner. Lean inward and firmly grasp hands with your partner.

Stretched Position—One partner either pulls strongly with his/her arms or leans backward to pull the other partner forward, stretching all the back muscles. Once one partner has fully stretched his/her back, he or she repeats the favor for the other partner.

Lower Back, Partner Stretch

Emphasis—Using this movement, you can stretch the lumbar muscles of your lower back.

Starting Position—Face your partner and stand far enough apart so you can both bend over and

Full Back, Partner Stretch (top, page 65).

Lower Back, Partner Stretch (middle, page 65).

Lower Back Stretch, (bottom, page 65).

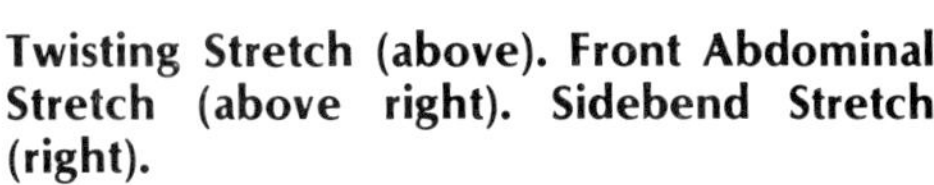

Twisting Stretch (above). Front Abdominal Stretch (above right). Sidebend Stretch (right).

intertwine your arms as illustrated. Keep your legs straight throughout the movement.

Stretched Position—Starting with your back slightly bent, arch it fully against your partner's resistance. Then provide your partner with resistance while he/she does the same movement. Alternate back and forth like this for each repetition.

Lower Back Stretch

Emphasis—As with the Lower Back, Partner Stretch, this movement will stretch and relax the lumbar muscles of your lower back.

Starting Position—Kneel down, bend your legs, and extend your arms directly forward. Round your back.

Stretched Position—From this position, arch your back fully and hold the arched position for the required number of seconds.

Twisting Stretch

Emphasis—This exercise stretches and tones the muscles at the sides of your waist.

Starting Position—Stand erect and place your hands together in front of your chest as illustrated. Maintain this hand position throughout the exercise.

Stretched Position—Trying to restrain the movement of your hips, twist your torso as far to the left or right as possible. Hold this position. Then twist as far to the other side as possible, hold, and repeat.

STRETCHING PROGRAM

Exercise	Emphasis	Starting Duration	Maximum Duration
1. Standing Hamstrings Stretch	Hamstrings	20 sec.	60 sec.
2. Hurdler's Stretch	Hamstrings/Hip Girdle	20 sec.	60 sec.
3. Seated Groin Stretch	Groin/Inner Thighs	20 sec.	60 sec.
4. Lunging Stretch	Hips/Thighs	20 sec.	60 sec.
5. Calf Stretch	Calves	20 sec.	60 sec.
6. Chest/Shoulder Stretch	Chest and Shoulders	20 sec.	60 sec.
7. Full Back Partner Stretch	Back	20 sec.	60 sec.
8. Twisting Stretch	Sides of Waist	20 sec.	60 sec.
9. Frontal Abdominal stretch	Front of Waist	20 sec.	60 sec.
10. Neck Stretches (all four directions)	Neck	20 sec.	60 sec.
11. Finger/Wrist Stretch (both sides)	Hands and Wrists	20 sec.	60 sec.

After 8–10 weeks of slow progression on the beginning program—and if you are particularly motivated to attain superior flexibility—you can try this more intense stretching routine (still do only one repetition of each movement):

Exercise	Emphasis	Maximum Duration
1. Standing Hamstrings Stretch	Hamstrings	90 sec.
2. Partner Hamstrings Stretch	Hamstrings	90 sec.
3. Hurdler's Stretch	Hamstrings/Hip Girdle	90 sec.
4. Seated Groin Stretch	Groin/Inner Thighs	90 sec.
5. Lunging Stretch	Hips/Thighs	90 sec.
6. Thigh Stretch (Standing)	Thighs	90 sec.
7. Calf Stretch	Calves	90 sec.
8. Chest/Shoulder Stretch	Chest and Shoulders	90 sec.
9. Full Back Partner Stretch	Back	90 sec.
10. Lower Back Partner Stretch	Lower Back	90 sec.
11. Sidebend Stretch	Sides of Waist	90 sec.
12. Frontal Abdominal Stretch	Front of Waist	90 sec.
13. Neck Stretches (all four directions)	Neck	60 sec.
14. Finger/Wrist Stretch (both sides)	Hands and Wrists	60 sec.

Front Abdominal Stretch

Emphasis—This movement stretches primarily the front abdominal muscles, but also the muscles of the hips and thighs.

Starting Position—Support yourself on straight arms and straight legs with your hips pointed upward so that your legs make an approximate 90-degree angle with your torso.

Stretched Position—Keeping your arms and legs straight, lower your hips as close to the floor (or beach) as possible. Hold this stretched position for the required number of seconds.

Sidebend Stretch

Emphasis—This exercise directly stretches the muscles at the sides of your waist.

Starting Position—Place your left hand on your

Front-to-Back Neck Stretch.

Side-to-Side Neck Stretch.

hip and extend your right arm overhead.

Stretched Position—As illustrated, lunge slightly to the right and bend at your waist as far to the left as possible.

Neck Stretch

Emphasis—These stretches influence all of the neck muscles.

Starting Position—Stand erect with your hands on your hips. Maintain this position with your legs, arms, and torso throughout the movement.

Stretched Position—Tilt your head as far forward as possible and hold this position. Then tilt your head as far backward as possible and hold that position. Next tilt your head as far to the right side as possible and hold that position. And finally tilt your head as far to the left side as possible and hold that position.

Palms-Out Finger/Wrist Stretch.

Finger/Wrist Stretch

Emphasis—These movements stretch all the muscles and joints of your fingers and wrists.

Starting Position—Stand erect and place the tips of your fingers together with your palms facing inward. As an alternative, you can place your fingers together with your palms facing outward.

Stretched Position—Press your wrists gently toward each other as illustrated.

Palms-In Finger/Wrist Stretch.

YOUR STRETCHING PROGRAM

As recommended under the heading "Stretching Progression," pick one exercise per body part and do not stretch to a point very close to your pain edge. Work up very slowly. The table on page 67 provides a good beginning stretching program that you can try (do one stretching repetition for each movement).

CONCLUSION

Here are the seven major points you should remember when following this stretching program:

1. Stretch every day, if possible.
2. Progress slowly (stretching must be a *gentle* form of exercise).
3. Take 30–40 seconds to ease into a stretch.
4. Find the pain edge and back off your stretch slightly. Hold the stretch for 30–90 seconds in this zone.
5. Do stretching exercises for every part of your body.
6. If you are an athlete, do your stretching program as a warm-up before a game or your regular workout. And if you have the time, repeat the stretching session as a warm-down following your game or training session.
7. Above all, try to make stretching an enjoyable part of your overall lifestyle.

With a few short weeks of faithfully following the stretching workouts I've outlined here, you'll notice a distinct improvement in your flexibility, health, physical fitness, athletic performance, and appearance. And within a few months you'll move as gracefully and appear as lean and fit as a jungle cat.

How to Develop Incredible Size and Strength!

by Roy Callender, as told to Bill Reynolds

Every bodybuilder I've met in the past 20 years has been waging a war to increase muscle mass and physical power. In bodybuilding, these two qualities go with the territory. Without power, you don't build mass; without sufficient density and mass, you can't hope to win a big title.

I discovered the relationship between mass and power early in my bodybuilding career. Simply put, there is a direct relationship between the size of your muscles and the weight you use in the basic exercises. The stronger you are in these exercises, the larger your muscles will be. I'm living proof of that.

Notice that I keyed in on *basic exercises,* the ones in which you work large muscle masses with heavy weights. Basic exercises also work more than one muscle group at a time, as opposed to *isolation exercises,* which work only a single muscle group, or occasionally only part of a muscle. Typical basic exercises are the Squat, Deadlift, Incline Press, Upright Row, and Barbell or T-Bar Bent Rowing.

When you are trying to build great muscle mass, it's useless to concentrate on isolation movements such as Concentration Curls and Leg Extensions. You simply can't handle enough weight in these movements to stimulate deep tissue growth and the ultimate in muscle mass. You will note that in my mass and power routine, which I'll outline later, I do no direct arm work whatsoever.

I have spent long periods doing mass and power training exclusively, but now I incorporate such work twice a week into my regular training schedule. I think this approach keeps me injury-free (or as close to that as possible), relieves boredom, and increases the power with which I do my normal exercises. I use mass and power training only in the off-season, however, because before a contest—what with strict dieting and all—I simply don't have the strength for it.

You'll have to be fairly well-advanced to handle this type of routine. It takes plenty of concentration to do it without running the risk of injury. There is also a great deal of pain that must be borne when training with extremely heavy weights. Most beginners can't handle that pain.

I always warm up thoroughly when power training, both at the beginning of each workout and before every exercise. When I'm training in California, where it's always warm, I can get by doing only two or three moderate warm-up sets. But in Canada, where the temperature can get pretty low, I have to do at least five or six progressively heavier warm-up sets before I tackle my heaviest weights in each exercise.

If you are having trouble acquiring muscle mass and additional strength, you probably should power train four days a week. You can pyramid your weights and reps, lowering the reps as you raise the poundage on progressive sets of each exercise. Here is an example of such a pyramid for the Squat (consider the first two or three sets as warm-ups):

Set Number	Weight	Reps
1	135	10
2	205	8
3	255	6
4	295	4
5	325	3
6	345	2

The table on page 72 provides a good four-day pyramid split routine (featuring basic exercises) that intermediate and slightly advanced bodybuilders can use to build additional mass and power.

As I mentioned, I've spent long periods training this way and I've had good results. But at the Olympian level, I need greater muscular detail, so I train for power only twice a week during the off-season. This usually involves very heavy workouts on Mondays when I am fresh from having rested on Sunday, and on Saturdays when I have a rest day ahead of me.

I don't count sets, but after my warm-up I probably do at most five or six sets per exercise. I do between two and five reps per movement, upping the weight each set.

ROY CALLENDER'S MASS/POWER PROGRAM

Day 1 (Mondays)

Extremely Heavy Calf Raises. All types, but most often the seated version. I use up to a half ton on the standing calf machine.

Squats. Up to 400–500 pounds. I don't like to go over 500, however, because my thighs are already big enough.

Leg Presses. I do these very strictly and slowly. Again, I don't go extremely heavy, because I don't wish to increase the mass of my thighs.

Deadlifts. I go up to only 450 pounds or so, not pushing too hard because I've had a serious back injury in the past. Deadlifts also improve my grip for such movements as Chins.

High Pulls. I use a grip slightly wider than my shoulders, and pull each rep from the floor up to my nose. It's almost like a Power Clean, except that I don't whip my elbows under the bar to catch it at my chest. I control the descent of the weight on each repetition.

Weighted Sit-Ups. I do only 3–4 sets here. You can't let your abdominals go when you're power training.

Day 2 (Saturdays)

Incline Dumbbell Presses. I go up to a pair of

Power-training increases strength in the basic exercises.

ROUTINE FOR INTERMEDIATE BODYBUILDERS

Monday & Thursday

Exercise	Sets	Reps
1. Incline Sit-Ups	2–3	20–30
2. Hyperextensions	2–3	15–20
3. Squats	6	10/8/6/4/3/2*
4. Deadlifts	3	5/4/3*
5. Barbell Bent Rowing	6	10/8/6/4/2*
6. Shrugs	4	10/8/6/4*
7. Barbell Curls	3	8/6/4*
8. Seated Calf Machine Toe Raises	5	10/8/6/5/4*

Tuesday & Friday

Exercise	Sets	Reps
1. Hanging Leg Raises	2–3	15–20
2. Incline Press	6	10/8/6/4/3/2*
3. Flat-Bench Flyes	3	8/6/4*
4. Military Presses	5	8/6/4/3/2*
5. Upright Rowing	4	8/6/4/3*
6. Lying Triceps Extension	3	8/6/4*
7. Standing Calf Machine Toe Raises	5	10/8/6/5/4*

*Pyramid the weights and reps on all movements marked with an asterisk.

150s; I prefer using dumbbells because they allow a greater range of motion than a barbell does.

Incline Flyes. My training poundage is a pair of 100s at the maximum; I'm working only my upper chest right now, because the lower part is very massive and I'm trying to balance my development.

Seated Press Behind Neck. I sit down with the weight after taking it off a Squat rack. I will go up to 215–225 pounds in this exercise and I'm very careful with my warm-ups. Last year, I had a persistent shoulder injury and was in agony while training for the Olympia. Now that the injury is healed, I don't want it to recur.

Side Laterals. I use a little cheat to get my 80-pound dumbbells up, but this is the only movement in which I use any cheating.

Partial Overhead Laterals. In this movement I use dumbbells weighing up to 110 pounds. The starting point of the movement is the finish position of the Dumbbell Press, except that the palms are inward. From this position I lower the dumbbells directly out to the sides until my arms are at about a 45-degree angle to each other, then I raise the dumbbells back to the starting point.

Upright Rows. I use a very close grip on this movement and go up to 175–185 pounds in very strict style.

T-Bar Rows. You should *never* cheat on this exercise, as I learned a couple of years ago when I severely injured my back doing the movement in loose form. I go up to 280 pounds for 3–4 reps.

Hanging Leg Raises. As with the Weighted Sit-Ups, I do only 3–4 sets. For increased resistance, I wear a pair of iron boots or hold a dumbbell between my feet.

While I do this routine twice a week during the off-season for increased muscle mass and physical power, I do my normal workout the other four days (I take Sundays off).

Six weeks before a competition, I begin training every day and drop the power training from my routine, although I still try to train fairly heavy on four or five basic exercises each workout. Such a training cycle is the main reason I was in such good shape at last year's Olympia.

Incidentally, I'm not unhappy that I lost at the 1981 Mr. Olympia. I was convinced that I was in the best possible condition for that stage of my career, and also that I was the best man onstage. Winning the contest itself wasn't as important to me as the personal satisfaction of achieving a perfect peak.

This year I will be training in California all year for the top contests. I'm preparing for the Pro Mr. Universe, all the Grand Prix competitions, the Gold Cup in South Africa, and the Olympia. By the end of the year, you simply won't believe how good I'll look!

My Arm Training Secrets

by Tim Belknap

When I started bodybuilding, I was a weak and puny teenager. I had just been released from the hospital after recovering from a bout with mononucleosis and jaundice. While I was in the hospital, my doctors also discovered that I had diabetes.

My illnesses left me very skinny. I tried gaining weight through diet, but had little success. So, in March of 1977, I joined a health club, hoping that weight training would beef up my body.

At that time my biceps were a mere 10″. Now, after four years of Weider-style training, I have built 20″ biceps and my overall arm development is tremendous.

A lot of bodybuilders wonder how I've been able to develop such massive arms in such a short time. Of course, bodybuilding success depends on hard work and discipline. But I have also developed some of my own training techniques that may help you to build mass all over your body, and particularly your arms.

I have found that to build biceps size and to develop an impressive horseshoe shape to the triceps I need to work with heavy poundages that really make the muscles burn. Because I train so heavily, I only need to do a total of nine sets for my triceps and nine sets for my biceps. And I only have to train my arms twice per week.

TRICEPS

I start my arm workout with three sets (8–10 reps per set) of Lying Triceps Extensions. One of my secrets is to do this exercise on a low decline, instead of lying on a flat exercise bench. This gives my triceps a greater initial stretch, as well as a more complete contraction at the finish position of the movement.

Another of my secrets is to use a rather narrow grip when doing Lying Triceps Extensions. By keeping my hands six inches apart, I can bring the bar closer to my forehead and work the triceps over a greater range of motion.

Next, I do three sets (8–10 reps per set) of Triceps Cable Pushdowns. I have a secret technique that makes this exercise even more effective for achieving both mass and definition. Most people do this type of Pushdown while standing perfectly erect. They push the bar straight down, keeping the elbows close to the body. I personally take a step back from the vertical line of the pulley and push down on the bar from that position, aiming for my feet. This gives my triceps a better stretch and a more complete contraction.

I also use a narrow grip in this exercise, and I prefer a straight bar to a V-bar. This method of doing Cable Pushdowns is especially good for building up the outer head of the triceps.

My final triceps exercise is One-Arm Triceps Extensions behind my head, using a dumbbell. The vertical position of my arm gives a maximum stretch to my triceps at the start of the movement. Again, I use very heavy poundages and concentrate on lowering the weight to the point of maximum triceps stretch. Then I press the dumbbell in a cantilever fashion and lock my arm straight to finish each rep. I do three sets of 8–10 repetitions for each arm, which finishes off my triceps routine.

Between all of my sets, I constantly flex my triceps in a variety of positions. I continue this technique (the Weider Iso-Tension Contraction Training Principle) for about 30 seconds and then go right into my next set. By exerting such steady tension throughout my workout I feel I am working my triceps muscles to the maximum, and this is one way I achieve the muscle burn necessary for optimum development.

As a contest approaches I do the same triceps routine, but I slightly increase the overall training intensity. Sometimes I do a couple more reps per set, but generally I depend on modifying my diet, not my workouts, to bring out maximum muscularity.

BICEPS

From the very beginning of my bodybuilding career I have more or less followed the same biceps routine. I start by doing Standing Curls with an EZ-curl bar. I do three sets with as heavy poundages as I can handle in strict form. I do 12 repetitions on the first set to get the blood flowing in my biceps. Then I do 10 reps on my second set, using more weight, and eight reps on the last set with an even heavier barbell. I insist on doing every repetition in strict form.

One-Arm Triceps Extensions stress the long inner head of the triceps.

Standing Curl with EZ-Curl bar is the basic biceps bomber.

Sometimes I even lean against the wall when I do my Curls. Or I will use a Weider Arm Blaster, which concentrates all of the curling effort on my biceps.

I have found that Curls with an EZ-curl bar are excellent for building biceps mass. The partially supinated position of the hands strongly stresses the inner biceps. And by using the EZ-curl bar, I can curl as much as 225 pounds for eight reps.

At this point in my workout, my biceps are warmed up enough to exert maximum power without risk of injury. So I start my next exercise, Incline Curls, with 80-pound dumbbells, my top weight for that exercise. Then as my biceps tire, I decrease the weight a bit on the second and third sets.

When I do Incline Curls my palms are turned upward during the curling and lowering of the dumbbell, and my form is kept as strict as possible. This hand position enables me to build a peak on my biceps. As in all my exercises, I keep the poundages high. I do three sets (8–10 reps per set).

I follow the Incline Curls with 3–4 sets (8–10 reps per set) of Seated Concentration Curls for each arm. I do this movement with my palms completely supinated (turned upward and even slightly outward). This hand position enhances the development on the outside of my biceps peak.

Four weeks before a contest I will add Cable Curls to my routine, but otherwise my entire biceps workout consists of the three exercises

I've just discussed. There are no dead spots in the range of motion when you do Cable Curls. You feel the resistance from full extension to full contraction. This allows me to take full advantage of the Weider Slow Continuous Tension Training Principle. After only three sets (8–10 reps/set) my biceps are totally pumped.

The Cable Curl is an excellent exercise for building both size and shape, and it also seems to enhance my arm vascularity. It's perfect for putting the finishing touches on my biceps before a contest. I use only 50 pounds or so for my Cable Curls. This is an intense exercise requiring maximum mental involvement, and I can get a better "feel" with lighter poundages.

I hate to admit it, but I have actually been reduced to using as little as 10 pounds for each arm on Cable Curls just before a contest, when my energy has been nearly exhausted from dieting. I believe that the actual amount of weight you use is less important than how you perform the exercise in both a physical and mental sense. Still, I am mentally geared for using heavy poundages and I am constantly striving to increase the resistance I use in every exercise.

There are various other exercises you can do for the biceps. For example, the Straight-Bar Curl also builds mass. But I don't recommend this movement when you are striving for muscularity just before a contest. You should also give Alternate Dumbbell Curls a tryout.

FOREARMS

My forearm workout begins with Wrist Curls. I like to do this movement with either a barbell or a single dumbbell, resting my forearms across a bench. On each rep I actually let the bar roll down my fingers at the start of the movement. Then I use my fingers to curl the bar into my fists before I complete the Wrist Curl in a normal manner.

I superset my Wrist Curls with Barbell Reverse Curls. The Reverse Curls build the brachialis muscle under my biceps and the supernator muscles in my forearms. I do five such supersets, performing 10 reps per exercise.

My training techniques are much like those of Mike Mentzer and Casey Viator. In each exercise, I try to achieve maximum mental concentration and to use very heavy poundages because I believe that's the best way to build mass and size.

Of course, there are no real secrets when it comes to building a great physique. It will take time, maximum effort, and total dedication. And you must *believe* in your ability to succeed. I hope my arm-training techniques will help you attain bodybuilding success.

Cable Curls accentuate the biceps peak.

Bertil Fox's Enormous Biceps

by Rick Wayne

The second thing you notice about Bertil Fox is his unflagging reluctance to talk about matters relating to his anatomical dimensions. Word is that his upper arms can stretch the tape measure to an incredible 22 inches. And while I doubt anyone will ever get the opportunity to test the validity of that rumor, it is quite obvious that Bertil's arms—the first thing you notice—are at least as large as your average weekend jogger's thighs.

They are the most unforgettable feature of this physique that has become particularly famous for the harmonious blending of its mammoth parts. The body part you remember long after your initial encounter with the Fox. They demand special attention even when hidden beneath the leather jacket that was tailored specifically to hide them.

Face it, when you've acquired arms like Bertil's you had better be prepared for life in the goldfish bowl.

The trouble is, Bertil has never learned to cope with his peculiar predicament. He has tried disguising his form in baggy shirts, but they just magnify his gargantuan proportions. And a leather jacket gets low marks in Southern California most of the year weatherwise.

You there, with the 12-inch pipestems, you don't know how lucky you are not to have arms like Bertil's. Right?

Bertil has tried living as Howard Hughes. Like a recluse, I mean. Unfortunately, his apartment, comfortable as it undoubtedly is, does not feature the kind of equipment that Bertil must use in his day-to-day bodybuilding life. Twice daily he must sneak out to Don Peters Fitness Center in Reseda. En route to his car he must pass the communal swimming pool and the gorgeous ladies who insist on stopping him to admire his form, much to our man's chagrin.

Sometimes a male show-off will engage him in esoteric conversation about some bodybuilding event. And suddenly the rap will turn toward Bertil's own set of muscular equipment, to his intense embarrassment. It's tough being the best in the world.

So, lately, Bertil has discovered another route to his car. When no one is looking, he'll crawl out through his bedroom window, which overlooks the carport. It's not exactly the most dignified way out, but at least it allows him to get to the gym without being waylaid by those wonder women at the pool.

So how does a writer get the Fox to talk about his training procedures? How does one get him to divulge the secrets behind his mountainous arms?

Well, if you are as resourceful as someone I could mention, you become a full-fledged member of the Don Peters Fitness Center. And you study Bertil for days. Surreptitiously, of course. If you are sufficiently conniving, you'll probably discover before too long that Bertil is not all that adverse to talking *per se*. That it's talking about himself that drives him bonkers. And if you are particularly blessed with perspicacity, enough to be a star writer at Weider, let us say, then doubtless you'll discover that Bertil's favorite topic is 1960s bodybuilding.

Which, of course, is just another way of saying Larry Scott.

The Fox cut his bodybuilding teeth devouring everything written about Scott. Thanks to Larry, Bertil learned early that well-built calves were a vital part of the competitive bodybuilder's armory. Early in his career Bertil decided against the theory that black bodybuilders were genetically limited in certain body parts. And thanks to the gospel according to Larry Scott, Bertil never favored one muscle over another. Every section of his physique received its full quota of torture.

But there was no denying the fact that, in the 1960s, Larry Scott's biceps were the most discussed phenomena in bodybuilding. True, you admired his massive thighs, the beautiful sweep of the calves, and the poses that were Scott's alone. But you could barely take your eyes off the Scott biceps. They were nothing at all like any you'd seen before.

Scott's biceps were a wonder to behold. Unique, incredibly thick and well-defined, they extended all the way from the shoulder to the elbow joint. Under tension, they rose high above the humerus. But not like an upended egg. No. Scott's biceps curved gradually to form a magnificent mound. If one has difficulty describing the muscle adequately, perhaps that's because it was finally ineffable. You had to see it to believe it.

During peak contraction on Concentration Curls, tense your biceps hard for 2–3 seconds.

And that Bertil did, in 1966, when Scott made his first trip to London. It seemed half the city turned out to see bodybuilding's golden boy that day. And Bertil came away more than ever determined to own a set of Scott model biceps.

There is no doubt he has succeeded. Look at his pictures. How did Bertil do it? Well, there was that little matter of the right genes. True enough. But his training procedures played the important role.

He trains his upper arms three times a week. The actual exercises hardly vary, although he tends to train faster in the last few weeks before a contest. He believes in heavy weights. Like Scott, he will not waste his energy on what he considers pansy dumbbells.

Ordinarily, Bertil trains his upper arms immediately after completing his deltoid

workout. Before a contest, however, when he is training twice daily using the Weider Double-Split Training Principle, he devotes a whole session to his biceps and triceps. Once in a while, for the sake of variety, he will do supersets. But he prefers to complete six sets of each exercise before moving on to the next.

Bertil's favorite barbell exercise for his biceps is done with a cambered bar. Occasionally, however, he uses a regular straight bar for the movement.

His training style as he does the regular Barbell Cheat Curl (with cambered or straight) bar) is best described as loose. The weight is swung to the shoulders, but that does not mean Bertil resorts to a kind of reversed clean to get the weight to his shoulders. He has developed such control that, even though he seems to be swinging the weight upwards, his biceps are fully engaged in the action. The weight is lowered as slowly as possible when you're working with a barbell that weighs more than 200 pounds.

As with all other biceps exercises, Bertil does six sets of 6–8 reps. He does not rush his sets. He takes as much rest as his instincts dictate. If he's feeling particularly peppy during a workout, then he'll take hardly any rest between sets. If not, he'll take his time.

His second biceps exercise is the two-arm Dumbbell Curl while seated on an incline bench. He starts with 70-pound dumbbells and works up to a pair of 100-pounders. Here he depends on his training partner to get the weight to his shoulders, and also in his deliberate lowering of the dumbbells. His concentration is particularly intense during the second phase of the exercise. Each succeeding set he increases the weight.

Compared with the weights used earlier, the poundage for Bertil's Concentration Curl is light. In fact, he uses a dumbbell weighing 50–60 pounds. He does the Concentration Curl from either a seated position or standing with his free hand supported on an exercise bench. Whichever style he uses, he makes a point of curling the weight slowly to his shoulders, then lowering it in a very controlled manner. He says he never thinks about the weight when he's performing the Bent-Over Concentration Curl. He concerns himself strictly with the action of the biceps throughout the movement. Here's how he puts it:

"I grab the weight and then, even before I start the Curl, I flex my biceps hard. Now I curl the weight slowly, never once relaxing the tension. I maintain the contraction as I slowly lower the weight to starting position."

It is little wonder that at the end of eight repetitions Bertil grimaces at the message from his biceps. The bentover concentration curl with a dumbbell is, by Bertil's account, the movement most responsible for the split-ball effect of his biceps.

Next comes the Preacher Curl, which Bertil calls the Scott Curl. Here he makes a point of allowing his elbows to extend about an inch past the bottom of the preacher board. From there he violently pulls the bar up to his shoulders, stops (without relaxing his biceps!), then slowly lowers to starting position. Here he relaxes completely before doing the next repetition. As noted, each exercise is done for 6–8 reps, in sets of six.

The One-Arm Cable Curl is fast challenging the Barbell Curl for that special spot in Bertil's heart. It's a movement that Bertil picked up from Joe Weider. And it has done wonders for Bertil's biceps.

The movement is similar to the dumbbell Bent-Over Curl, except for two points: one, it's performed while standing. And two, as Bertil curls the weight, he gradually twists his wrist outwards, thereby placing extreme stress on the outer head of his biceps. His wrist is kept straight as he lowers the weight. Here again, Bertil trains with maximum poundage—as much as he can manage. And the movement is fairly strict.

For those who wish to know, Bertil always trains his biceps and triceps during the same session. He starts with the triceps and finishes off with the routine featured here.

When he trains arms and shoulders in the same session, shoulders come first, then triceps, followed by biceps.

Beginners hardly need be reminded that Bertil's workout is not designed for them. He recommends just two each for biceps and triceps exercises, three sets each movement, for newcomers.

It's worth mentioning here that Bertil was himself amazed at the improvement in his arms after only a few weeks under Joe Weider's direction. Thanks to the Master Blaster, he now has a better understanding of the Weider System, which produced Scott and the other champions Bertil admired in the 1960s. More than ever he has learned to trust his instincts. And he has become particularly discriminating in his choice of exercises.

Titanic Triceps

by Mike Mentzer

What's your favorite pose? Which one do you like to see your favorite muscle star doing? Is it the double biceps, the lat spread, the infamous "crab," or perhaps you prefer the more ethereal Zane-type poses—with arms overhead, open hands pleading. Not me. I've always gone in for the simplest pose of all, the pose of repose (i.e., standing relaxed).

I'll never forget the first time I saw the Leo Stern series of photos taken of Bill Pearl in relaxed positions. The most striking thing about these photos, whether they were taken from the front, side, or, yes, even the back, was Pearl's hamhock of a triceps. I mean, there was no hiding it; whatever the angle of vision, his triceps were so imposing.

Impressive triceps development is nice to have not only for the posing platform, but for everyday appearance as well. Let's face it, most of our time is spent in a relaxed, arms-at-our-sides position. In this position, it's a well-developed triceps that gives the arm an impressive look.

TRICEPS FUNCTION AND DESIGN

Understanding which exercises are best for

stimulating full triceps development requires a knowledge of the anatomy and function of the muscle. The word *triceps* derives from the Latin; it means three heads. The triceps has an inner, outer, and middle head. The primary function of the triceps is to straighten the arm. Its secondary function is to bring the upper arm into the body. The most productive exercises for the triceps, therefore, are those that provide resistance as the muscle performs these two functions.

The two conventional-equipment exercises which come closest to being full-range triceps movements are the Pressdown on the lat machine and the Parallel Bar Dip. Although other exercises can be performed, these two should constitute the core of your triceps routine.

Many people ask: In what order should one train the respective body parts? A rule of thumb is: *Always train your largest muscle groups first* since they demand more energy and, obviously, you have more energy at the start of your workout. It's especially important that you always train your biceps and triceps after working the muscles of the torso. The triceps, for example, is involved in many of the pressing movements used in training the delts and pecs. So always train triceps *after* delts and pecs. Why limit the weight and intensity of your delt and pec training by fatiguing and weakening the triceps first?

Since the triceps receive so much direct stimulation from pressing movements, you should also be sure to limit the number of sets of triceps work, doing no more than five sets twice a week. I usually train my triceps on Monday and Thursday after completing my chest and delt work.

Every rep of every set I perform for my triceps—or for any other muscle for that matter—is done deliberately and under full control. Starting an exercise with a sudden jerk and continuing rapidly to completion applies resistance only at the start and end of the movement. Yanking and jerking weights out of the starting or extended position is also traumatic to joints and connective tissue. By initiating all movements deliberately and under full control, resistance is applied evenly through the full range of motion. This results in more balanced development of the muscle and reduces the chances of injury.

I also emphasize the lowering phase of each rep. This not only ensures control, but it makes the exercise much more effective. Many exercise physiologists believe that negative work (i.e., lowering of the weights) is the most productive part of a rep.

EXERCISES

Pressdown

This exercise is very valuable because it requires that the triceps performs both of its functions: straightening the arms and keeping the upper arms close to the body. Do the exercise with your hands held shoulder width apart (or slightly closer) and the elbows perfectly stationary at your sides. *Do not* allow your elbows to travel away from your sides; if the elbows go out wide, your pecs and lats come into play.

Begin the movement deliberately from the extended position and continue by straightening the arms until the elbows are fully locked. When the arms are in the locked position, make an effort to pull the bar as close to your body as possible. Pause momentarily in this position and then lower the weight slowly and under full muscular control.

After I've done 6–8 reps in this fashion, my partner will help me force out two or three more reps in which I exaggerate the reverse-gravity portion even more, taking up to four seconds to lower the weight. Then, taking no rest at all, I proceed directly to the next exercise.

Dips

After exhausting my triceps in the Pressdowns, I go to a compound exercise, such as Dips, which allows me to continue working my triceps "beyond normal failure" by utilizing my front delts and pecs.

When doing Dips for the triceps, be sure to keep the elbows tucked in as close to the body as possible. Although I usually perform six reps to positive failure, then continue with several forced and negative reps, every third workout or so I proceed from Pressdowns to Dips done in purely negative fashion (i.e., I do no positive reps—raising the body—at all). I stand on a bench that allows me to start in the top or peak contracted position. From there I lower myself very slowly all the way to the bottom. I then stand up on the bench and lower once more. I will do this five or six times.

Performing Dips in this fashion, be sure to use a weight that allows you to lower yourself all the way to the bottom under full control. If you find yourself dropping quickly into the bottom position after you reach the halfway point, the weight you're using is too heavy.

Occasionally I will also start a triceps workout with Dips so that I can use heavier weights.

Barbell or Nautilus Extensions

For variety I will often include a set or two of either Barbell Extensions, Nautilus Extensions, or maybe a set of each. Perform Lying Barbell Extensions with the head over the edge of the bench so that the triceps can achieve greater extension. Keep the elbows tucked in as close as possible and directly over the throat. Lower the bar slowly to the throat, pause, and with no sudden jerk or thrust, "muscle" the weight back to the top.

Fight the tendency in this exercise to jerk the weights from the extended position when it starts to feel very heavy around the fifth or sixth rep. The joints and tendons in the extended position are particularly vulnerable and such a sudden thrust could result in tendinitis or even a tear.

Again, I will perform 6–8 reps, plus one or two forced reps, and once a week I will include negatives.

TRICEPS ROUTINE

Here is the triceps routine I recommend:

1. Triceps Pressdowns supersetted with . . .
2. Parallel Bar Dips (One or two supersets of 6–8 reps, plus two forced reps. Once a week or so add negatives.)
3. Barbell Extensions (lying down)—One or two sets of 6–8 reps.
4. Nautilus Extensions—One or two sets of 6–8 reps.

Let me point out that this is merely a suggested routine. Feel free to vary it if you wish. In some workouts you might want to start with heavy Dips (after a good warm-up), then do a superset of Pressdowns and Dips. On other occasions you might substitute the Lying Barbell Extensions or Nautilus Extensions for the Triceps Pressdowns. There are many ways of mixing up the routine for variety.

Beginners need not perform the forced and negative reps for at least the first 3–6 months. Going to positive failure (where they can no longer raise the weight) should provide enough stimulus for their relatively untrained muscles. But after 6–12 months they should add the forced reps and negative (reverse-gravity) movements since their muscles will require more intensity to grow. No one, and that includes advanced bodybuilders, should do negatives and forced reps every workout.

Tom Platz Goes to the Biceps-Blasting Limit!

by Bill Dobbins

Most young bodybuilders fall into a trap—they get carried away training the chest and arms and neglect the rest of the body, especially the legs. The first two body parts seem to them to represent the epitome of strength and manliness: the macho muscles. You see it all the time in the gym. It happened to Arnold Schwarzenegger when he was a kid training in Austria. It happened to Larry Jackson, Tony Pearson and a lot of others. But this was not the case with young Tom Platz. For him, it was almost the opposite.

"From the time I was 14," Tom says, "I was training mostly with weightlifters. So I was less interested in arms and chest. When you're training for competitive weightlifting, the areas you have to concentrate on the most are the legs and trunk."

But Tom always had it in his mind to become a bodybuilder. So he did not neglect the rest of his body entirely. But, he admits, when it came to training arms, his heart simply was not in it.

"I did arm training," Tom recalls, "but I was never able to get the same feeling I got when I worked legs. I would do legs, really heavy Squats, and try to follow with arm training. But I was already tired and a lot of the time I found myself just going through the motions."

Even with the heavy poundages weightlifters use in training, they don't get the arm development bodybuilders need. Heavy Cleans, for example, involve the biceps, but don't give them the full range of motion that creates great arms. And, while pressing works the triceps, it represents only one limited type of movement and doesn't create an arm with a true bodybuilding shape.

"When I came out to California," Platz says, "everything changed. I had gotten into weightlifting originally to get thicker and denser so I would be better at bodybuilding. Now I was among bodybuilders whose workouts involved a lot of arm training, so I found myself doing Curls instead of Power Cleans."

Since then, Tom's arms have improved a great deal and are on their way to becoming one of his best body parts. But before he could get the most out of his arm training, first Tom sought the mental connection that would allow him to train his arms with the same intensity he had always put into his legs.

"Joe Weider told me many times, 'Every body part is an emotion.' That always made a lot of sense to me. I have a different feeling, a different emotion with each body part. I had some trouble developing this feeling for triceps. For example, mastering Triceps Pushdowns took me a long time.

"Whenever I think about arms," Tom continues, "I can see the photo of Arnold on the cover of *Education of a Bodybuilder*—that phenomenal biceps peak, a mountainous arm with mountains in the background. I could stare at that photo for hours." But once Tom actually starts training he doesn't use visualized images to focus his attention. He concentrates on the Weider Slow-Continuous Tension Training Principle, feeling the muscle working through its range of motion. It is this feeling, this direct connection between mind and muscle, that Tom believes is the key to total intensity.

TOM PLATZ'S ARM WORKOUT

Superset: Standing Alternate Dumbbell Curls and Close-Grip Bench Presses
Seated French Presses
Standing Barbell Curls
Triceps Pushdowns
Wrist Curls
(In off-season: Weighted Dips instead of Close-Grip Presses)

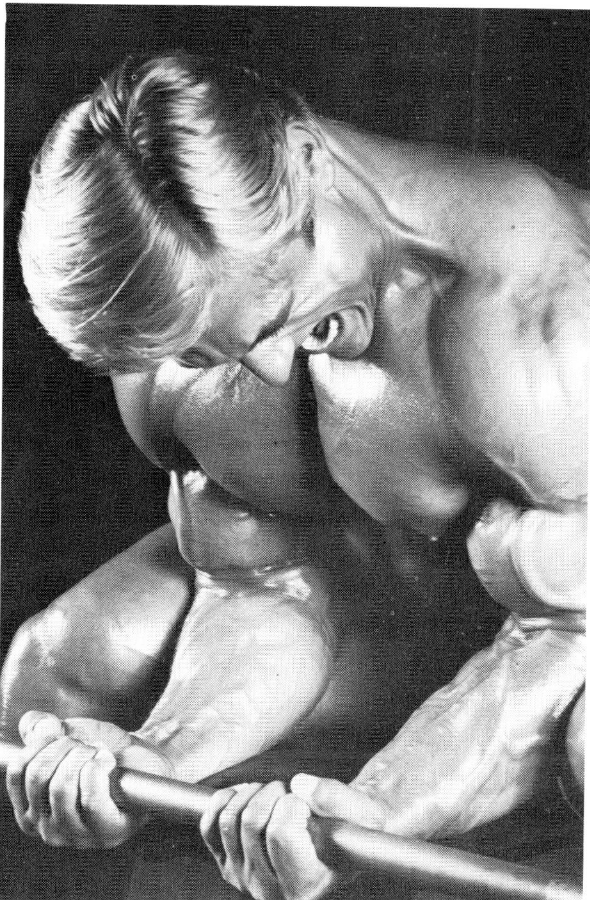

Wrist Curls, when done with arms running along the top of a bench, are an extremely intense forearm movement.

"I get extra intensity in my arm training by using the Weider Priority System," Platz explains. "I train arms by themselves, no other body parts, so that I can give them my full attention.

"Some bodybuilders say you don't need much arm training since training back and chest involves the biceps and triceps. But when I am rowing or doing heavy Presses, my mind isn't into arms. And when my mind is not involved, I don't get much response from the muscles. So I have to do a separate training session just for arms.

"Even so, the biceps and triceps are very small muscles. If you train them really hard, put a lot of intensity into the workout, I don't see how you can do more than about 10 sets for each muscle. If you can do more, you aren't training hard enough."

Tom begins by supersetting Alternate Dumbbell Curls and Close-Grip Bench Presses with an EZ-curl bar. "I don't get much out of heavy Barbell Curls with a lot of cheating—I need to feel the exercise more strictly."

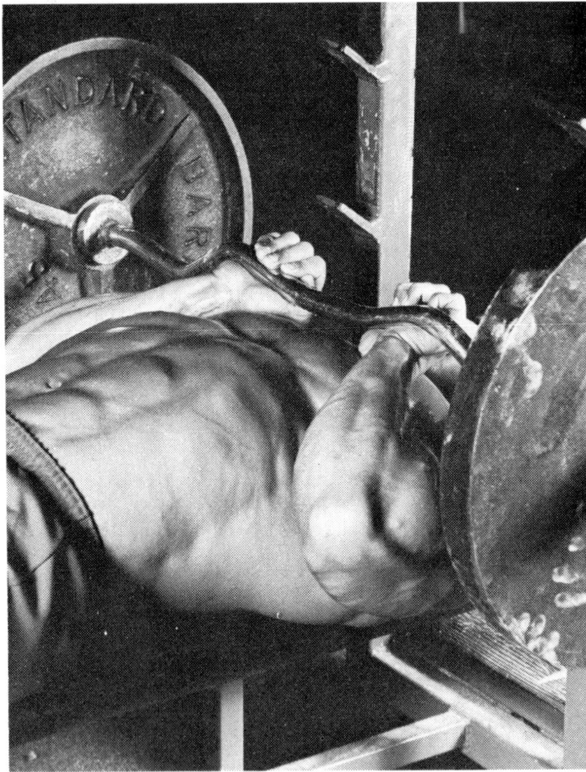

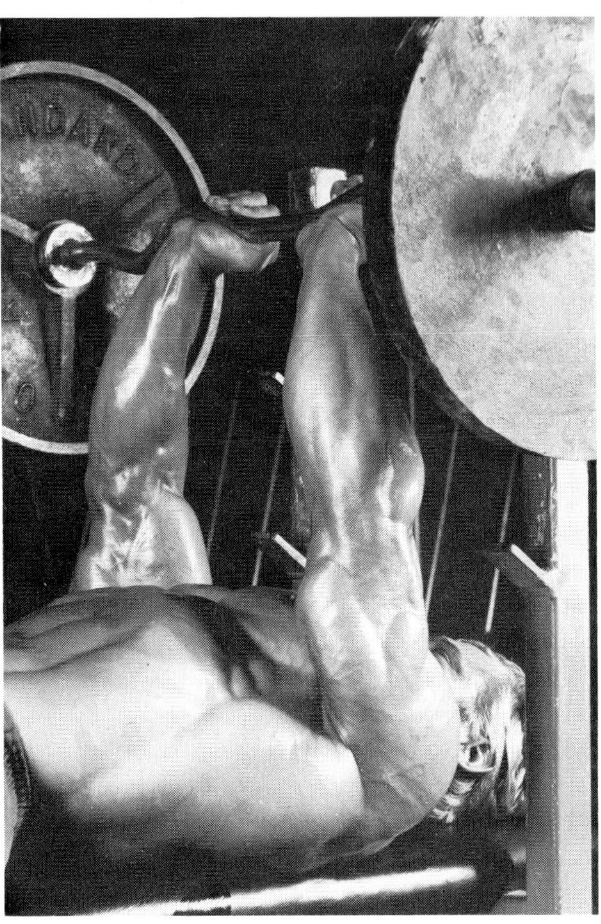

Platz recalls how he used to go into the gym early in the morning when nobody else was around, take 20-pound dumbbells, and do very strict Curls until he mastered the Isolation Principle, making the biceps do all the work. He gradually increased the weight until now he can use 70-pound dumbbells and get the same feeling and the same strict movement.

"When I'm not training for competition," he adds, "I drop the Close-Grip Presses and do very heavy Weighted Dips instead." Tom normally does his Dips with a 135-pound dumbbell fastened to his waist—heavy ènough to work his triceps, but not too heavy so that he can't get in sufficient reps. When he is too exhausted to continue, he lifts himself up, locks out his arms, and holds this position as long as he can.

Following the superset, Tom does Seated French Presses, but even here he has a twist: as he lowers the weight behind his head, he has his training partner force the bar down as far as possible, stretching the triceps to the absolute maximum.

"This adds a whole other dimension to the exercise," Tom says.

Tom does his Standing Barbell Curls very slowly and strictly. Again, contrary to bodybuilders such as Franco Columbu and Arnold Schwarzenegger, who like to do heavy Cheat Curls, Tom simply doesn't enjoy the way they feel. He prefers to keep the bar totally under control and concentrate on how the biceps feel throughout the longest range of motion possible.

For Triceps Pushdowns, Tom uses a straight bar. This allows him to feel the exercise more in the triceps than with a V-shaped one. He does the movement strictly, locking his arms out fully at the bottom of the movement and, at the top, having his training partner press down on the weight stack to stretch his triceps to the maximum.

"I do Wrist Curls just the way Arnold does," Tom explains, "forearms along a bench, letting the weight roll down into the fingers, then curling the bar up as far as I can." After years of heavy Power Cleans, Tom doesn't feel his forearms need any Reverse Curls to bring out extra development.

Tom was quite happy with the way his arms looked at the 1981 Olympia, but he still isn't completely satisfied. "I'm not willing to put limits on myself," he says.

And so he is still interested in developing more fullness in the triceps, which may require

adding more exercises to his off-season training program. He still has in his mind's eye that vision of Arnold's arm with its massive biceps peak. That remains a goal.

"Off-season, when I'm training for maximum size, I train slower, with less an aerobic demand, and I cut out the supersets. However, as I've said before, the irony of the whole thing is the more successful you get in bodybuilding—the more exhibitions, seminars, and personal appearances you do—the less time you have for training.

"But I'll tell you one thing—I want to be Mr. Olympia. And I won't let anything interfere with that. If winning the Olympia means I have to develop the world's best arms, then I'll develop the world's best arms. I believe that the only limitations that affect me are the ones I impose on myself."

The Back

by Tim Belknap

Back development, although so important to success in bodybuilding contests, is the most common weakness among competitive bodybuilders. Too often body fat covers existing development. I knew I couldn't afford that kind of flaw. I realized I had to have a back that was absolutely shredded if I was to win the big contests. I knew I had to build total muscularity and could never allow body fat to hide it.

When I train my back, I work very hard, using a lot of mental concentration, muscle tensing, and posing. After a back workout I do as many as 10 sets of tension posing, using the back double biceps pose seen in competition (I hold the pose about 12 seconds). Each set is followed by stretching exercises, such as hanging from a chinning bar or pulling against a stationary upright.

It takes me about 40 minutes to complete a back workout. I do my chest training during the day, and my back work in the evening. I make use of the popular Double-Split Training Principle, working each body part twice a week, but concentrating on different muscle groups on different days. My back used to be considered my weak point, but not anymore. They say my back was spectacular when I won the 1981 Mr. America contest.

I start my back routine with five very heavy sets of Seated Rows, done on a special rowing machine in Gold's Gym. I perform each rep to full peak contraction, and there's no way to cheat on that. I do 10 repetitions on all the exercises.

Next I do 3–4 sets of Pulldowns to the chest, using a semiwide grip. I work heavy, and whether I do three sets or four sets depends entirely on my energy level. The energy factor is critical when I am down to 900 calories a day the last four weeks before a contest.

Then I do close-grip Pulldowns to the chest, using a reverse grip, 3–4 sets. This exercise strikes deep into the lower lats.

For my final pulldown exercise I do wide-grip Chins behind the neck, 3–4 sets. I pull deep on all these exercises, pausing at the bottom of each rep, forcing the muscle to peak contract. This makes a total of 10 or 11 sets of pulldown movements.

I finish with two sets of heavy dumbbell Pullovers. And that's my complete back workout. I don't do stiff-legged Deadlifts or the like.

With my diabetes, it's hard for me to train early in the morning. It takes me a while to get my blood sugar level up, so I work my chest about 1 pm, and after sunbathing and resting, return to the gym about 8 pm for my back workout.

I do a lot of tension posing to bring out that extra muscularity. For the Mr. America I went from 223 pounds three-and-a-half weeks before the show, all the way down to 191 the day of the contest. I don't know if I will ever do that, or have to do that, again. I accomplished that through diet and my new method of training. Perhaps it was overkill, but I got the muscularity I wanted.

I attribute a great deal of my muscularity to tension posing. Between sets I do many different back poses. In fact, the time between sets does not constitute a rest period for me because I use it for tension posing. There is no way of calculating how much energy I expend on it, but I would guess it is an enormous amount, perhaps equal to that used on actual exercises. I had always read about it, and I remember how much Joe Weider stressed it (the Iso-Tension Training Principle). Feeling its effectiveness was a revelation.

As I do the double biceps back pose, I turn my head from side to side to bring more of the trapezius muscles into the movement. I keep my back straight, tensing the spinal erectors and

lumbars. I now have transverse striations that appear across the lower half of my back, depending on how I shift my poses and on how I direct tension to that area.

I keep mentioning how hard I work, especially when zeroing in on competition, or even for an exhibition. I sometimes wonder what drives me, and I am amazed at my capacity for effort. That's all it is—no miracle drug or anything—just hard work.

I depend a lot on instinctive training. Some days I am more tired than others. Other days I have more energy and can hold my tension poses longer. I try not to rush my workouts, although I do go through them rather fast. I complete the back workout in 40 minutes, and spend about the same amount of time on my chest—a total of one hour and 20 minutes for my hardest training day. Since I work individual body parts twice a week, that means I have two extremely hard workouts a week. I train seven days a week.

One day a week, usually Sunday, I work miscellaneous body parts, like lower back and abdominals. I continue to do the same exercises, but change the intensity as a contest nears.

Unquestionably, my diet is intense. You have to diet to bring out full muscular detail. For the Mr. America show I lost 32 pounds in a few weeks. I am often asked how I could lose so much in so short a period, but I am sure a lot of it was water weight. I was hard, ripped, and muscular. Diet was largely responsible. I was shocked when they weighed me in at 191. I thought at first they were wrong.

I don't feel I lost too much too fast, although I was hungry all the way. I was starving myself and felt terrible. I was getting 90 grams of protein a day at the most. I kept my carbohydrate intake fairly high, staying within the daily 900-calorie limit. I kept my protein intake low; protein is for building muscle during the early stages of contest training, but not for cutting up during the final few weeks.

I like to do a fast-paced workout, getting in as much work as I can in the least amount of time. I don't like to talk in the gym; I prefer to go in, get the job done, and get out. In that way you don't get stale or bored with training.

I also favor very heavy, high-intensity weight training. Of course, that is hard to do on a stringent diet, but I guess that's where determination comes in.

I wouldn't recommend my very advanced

weight-training program for a newcomer. The diet alone would have you twisting slowly in the wind. I started the diet four-and-a-half weeks before the show, but I didn't plunge in all at once. I took it gradually, paring my food intake as I went along, getting accustomed to the deprivation.

Those transverse cuts across the lower part of my back came as the result of diet. I planned it that way. The muscle was always there, the product of my continual heavy back training. The tension posing and Hyperextensions did the rest.

I do Hyperextensions as part of my midsection training, but they also double as lower back work. I hold a 30-pound weight behind my head and do three sets of 30 reps, holding each rep at the top, feeling the tension build up in my lumbars. That's a lot of weight and repetitions on that exercise. I concentrate on doing the exercise from a starting position with my trunk only a few inches below horizontal, and come up to the full hyperextension position. Lowering the head to the floor is a waste of motion. The short range of motion at the high end of the movement provides the work and tension necessary for maximum development.

If you look at most bodybuilders competing today, you'll notice that the weakest areas tend to be the lower abdominals and the lower back. Unfortunately, these bodybuilders don't seem to consider them important areas and fail to work them as hard as other body parts. I believe these areas can be deciding factors in a contest. Too frequently I see contestants with fat on their lower abdominals and lower back. To me that's not a complete physique. You have to be totally cut *everywhere*. It's easy to get your chest and arms cut and keep them that way because fat doesn't accumulate much in those areas. The first place in which I accumulate fat is on my obliques and lower back. When I hold the double biceps pose in my tension work, I rock slightly from side to side, tensing the obliques and lumbars on each side.

It seems you have to resort to extreme measures in bodybuilding. A lot of guys think I'm crazy for constantly training so heavily, but I wouldn't feel good about myself if I didn't make every effort to achieve maximum results. Sometimes I feel like throwing in the towel, but I don't. I keep going because there is so much to do, and so very little time. I can't compromise perfection. It's perfection that wins.

Row, Row, Row Your Lats!

by Charles Fraser

The galley slaves of ancient Rome pulled the oars that helped the Romans rule their empire. The slaves who survived developed powerful back muscles—particularly the latissimus dorsi, which gives the upper body the flaring **V** shape.

Victor Hugo's classic *Les Miserables* is the story of Jean Valjean, who was sentenced to 19 years in the galleys because he stole a loaf of bread to feed his sister's starving family. After the convict's release, his relentless enemy, Inspector Javert, finds Valjean living under an assumed name, the respected mayor of a town in northern France. Valjean gives himself away by saving the life of a man pinned under a heavy cart. Javert then notices the mayor's powerful back muscles and is convinced that he developed them chained to an oar in the galleys.

Fortunately the reader doesn't have to be a convict to develop these majestic muscles that identify him or her as a bodybuilder. The wings of humankind! What beautiful and commanding things are these flaring muscles that extend from the armpit to the waist! They are the largest muscles of the upper body. They, more than any other muscle, determine how big and developed the torso looks.

Years ago this writer had the pleasure of having supper with the great Russian ballet dancer, Rudolph Nureyev. When I told him that he would look more imposing onstage if he developed his upper body, his eyes lit up with intense interest. He was eager to learn how he might improve his already great presence. I told him to get a barbell or join a gym and do several sets of Bent-Over Rows for the lats and Presses for the shoulders. He said he would get going as soon as he returned to London. I encourage other performers to follow this simple advice in their search for charisma.

While rowing a boat does develop the lats and gives you upper-body stamina, the high repetitions and relatively low resistance involved does not permit the oarsman to develop the lat width and thickness that a bodybuilder usually has. But it's the *movement* of rowing that develops the lats and allied back muscles. The lats can be very well developed by doing Chins, but the rowing motion can bring greater back thickness and develop the spinal erector muscles as well.

To do most rowing exercises, you have to bend forward with the back parallel to the floor.

In this position the erector muscles along the spine must resist the pull of the weight being used. Therefore, rowing develops the spinal erectors.

One advantage of the rowing motion is that it can be done without any special equipment. Anyone who has a barbell can do it.

Rowing is a compound movement involving more than one set of joints. Rowing moves the shoulder and elbow joints. The hip-waist bend puts stress not only on the spinal erectors, but the gluteus as well. In addition, the legs are used as stabilizers. All in all, any more than one or two sets of rowing motions becomes hard work. Doing several sets of heavy Rows will induce heavy breathing and sweating. And don't forget that rowing also develops the brachialis, biceps, forearms, and hands. All of this makes rowing one of the four or five basic exercises of bodybuilding.

The rowing motion is one of those exercises that clearly demonstrate the vast superiority of weight training over calisthenics. Enthusiastic instructors of calisthenics have their charges do Push-Ups. But weights or some kind of resistance apparatus is necessary to work the pulling muscles.

For the bodybuilder who is fond of doing Bench Presses and Flyes, some form of rowing is a must. Rowing is the opposite or antagonistic movement to all bench pressing and pectoral exercises that bring the arms forward. Rowing brings the arms back.

GENERAL ROWING INSTRUCTIONS

There are certain techniques that should be used in all rowing motions. Do the exercise at medium to slow speed. Concentrate on the lats, not the arms. When the elbows are in, or back as far as they will go, pause for a half second, contract the lats, then lower the arms slowly. Resist the weight as it descends. Never drop it. You will be missing almost half the value of the exercise if you don't fight gravity on the way down.

Keep the reps between six and ten. Include Rows in your training two or three times a week. If you do them three times a week, the middle workout should be lighter and less intense than the other two. This will help to prevent overtraining.

Work out with a steady rhythm. Rest only long enough for breathing to return to almost normal. For most beginners this will mean a rest of 1.5–2 minutes, for an intermediate about 60 seconds. An advanced bodybuilder may be able to rest as little as 30 seconds. Although some bodybuilders claim they rest less than 30 seconds, such short rests are impractical for muscle-building purposes. If you take too short a rest, you lose your intensity of effort and concentration.

Concentrate on doing strict, full reps, but once a week you can go "beyond failure" by doing a few partial reps. Another system to increase the intensity is to use the erector muscles of the back to impart a little "swing" to the movement. This will enable you to use more weight, or do more reps, but the weight should always be lowered slowly. This should be done at the end of the set when you can no longer do strict movements (the Weider Cheating Principle).

The number of sets to be performed should be determined by your length of experience as a bodybuilder. Here's a rough guide:

Absolute Beginner
One warm-up set, one working set per exercise.

Intermediate Beginner (one month of training)
One warm-up set, two working sets.

Intermediate (six months of training)
One warm-up set, three working sets.

Advanced (two years of training)
One warm-up set, four working sets.

The warm-up set should be performed with a weight 80–90% of the working set. Here are the major rowing exercises:

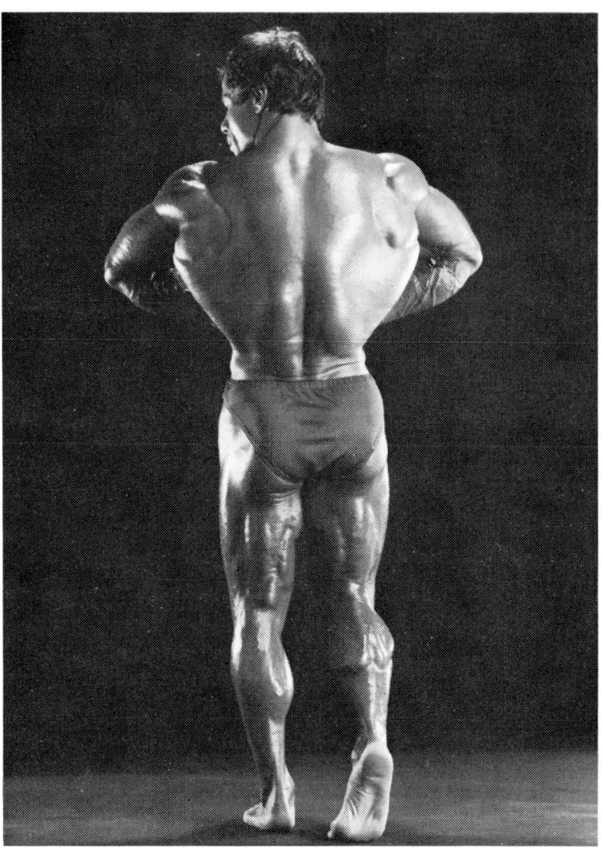

The incredible back of Franco Columbu.

REGULAR BARBELL ROW

This is the basic staple of rowing. If you use an Olympic bar with the large 45-pound plates, the diameter of the plates likely will prevent you from doing a full movement—the plates will touch the floor before the full stretch position is reached. Therefore, use smaller plates or stand on a four-inch board or a sturdy box. The grip should be about shoulder-width or narrower. The hands should be pronated, knuckles away from the body. Bend the legs and pick up the barbell. With a slight bend of the knees, lean forward until your torso is parallel with the floor. Starting with the arms in the fully extended position, pull the barbell up to the lower chest. Hold briefly, contracting the arms and lats. Lower and repeat.

DUMBBELL ROW

The advantage of dumbbells is that they will force both sides to work equally. Also, the position of the hands can be varied. You can hold the dumbbells in the same position as a barbell, with the dumbbells parallel to each other, or at some other angle. Pull the dumbbells from the bottom position to the sides of the lower ribs. Hold in this position for a half-second and then lower slowly.

For variety and improvement of coordination, the dumbbells can be rowed alternately.

SEATED CABLE ROW

A Seated Cable Rowing apparatus is now available in most well-equipped gyms. Ever since the movie *Pumping Iron,* which showed Ed Corney pumping out repetitions in the Seated Cable Row, this form of rowing has become more and more popular. The movement approximates the position and movement of an oarsman.

Cable Rows can be performed in two ways: with strict arm motion only or with the aid of the spinal erector muscles. Beginners and intermediates should start with strict form, bracing their feet against the foot bar, holding their torso perpendicular, and rowing. Later on the spinal erector motion can be used. The person starts by pulling with the erector muscles, then follows with a concentrated pulling of the lats and arms. Then the arms are straightened slowly, resisting the weight as it's returned to the extended position. Let the "cheating" of the erector motion merely enable you to use heavier weights; don't allow it to take the concentrated effort out of the lats.

ONE-END BARBELL ROW

Apparently this exercise began way back when some bodybuilder was looking for a different way to do Rows. He straddled the barbell and put his hands around the bar, one in front of the other against the inside collar. Then he pulled the plates at the end of the barbell up to his chest and lowered them. The next set he would switch hands. This kind of rowing motion allowed the exerciser to achieve the narrowest grip and, therefore, the most stretch. If large plates are used, they will touch the chest before a complete movement can be executed. This is okay. Heavier weights can be used to make the beginning and middle portion of the movement harder.

Most gyms have a One-End Bar Rowing apparatus. These bars have either a pair of parallel bars grips close together where the bar is gripped or a cross bar. There's a scene in *Pumping Iron* (here I go again) in which the camera catches Arnold Schwarzenegger from a low angle bending over the ponderously loaded bar and straining out repetitions while chewing gum at the same time. One Southern California bodybuilder told me it was his favorite scene in the movie. He always pictured it when he did this exercise. Again, this exercise can be done with rigid body position, or with some momentum imparted by the spinal erectors.

ONE-DUMBBELL ROW

This rowing exercise is especially useful for individuals with pulled muscles in the lower back. The One-Dumbbell Row can be done without placing stress on the erector muscles. The individual can support his torso with his free hand placed on a bench or against his thigh.

Here are some suggested rowing routines for bodybuilders:

Beginner

Regular Barbell Row—2 sets.

Intermediate Beginner

Regular Barbell Row—3 sets.
One-Arm Dumbbell Row—3 sets.

Intermediate

Regular Barbell Row—4 sets.
Dumbbell Row—3 sets.
Seated Cable Row—3 sets.

Advanced

Regular Barbell Row—4–5 sets.
One-End Barbell Row—4–5 sets.
Dumbbell Row—4 sets.
Cable Row—3–4 sets.

The advanced routine presented here is a lot of rowing. The routine can be reduced, especially if you do Chins for the lats in the same workout.

Constantly doing the rowing motion over the months and years will develop wide, thick latissimus dorsi muscles. As an aid to using more weight in rowing, I recommend Deadlifts. A combination of deadlifting and rowing will develop the ultimate back. Remember, Franco Columbu, of the great lats, is also a phenomenal deadlifter.

Row on and on, and someday you'll have the impressive lat development you want.

Amazing Thighs!

by Chris Dickerson

Yin and Yang. Light and dark. Good and bad. Beauty and ugliness. Everything in the world is in balance. And in the bodybuilding world everything must also be in balance—if you want to be a winner.

I've never had trouble developing my calves. My God, they were more than 16 inches in circumference before I had ever touched a weight! By comparison, my thighs were reed thin when I first walked into Bill Pearl's Gym in Pasadena, CA, and it's been a grueling battle for me to build them up so they're in balance with my calves. Over the years I've succeeded in attaining such balance, but the perspiration I've shed while working my thighs would probably fill a small lake.

The secret of my thigh development is that I do as many sets for that muscle group as I do for my back and chest. Too many young bodybuilders do four sets of Squats, three sets of Leg Extensions, and three sets of Leg Curls, believing this series of exercises comprises a thigh workout. Then they wonder why my thighs are so much better than theirs. Well, let me clue you in on the reason for my success—I do *three times* as much thigh work as the bodybuilders I've just mentioned.

Thigh training is undeniably painful. The thigh muscles are the largest in the body. When fatigue toxins start building up in your thighs partway through a set of Squats, you feel like someone is going at your legs with a flamethrower. When Joe Weider coined his now-famous "no pain, no gain" maxim, he must have had thigh training in mind. No one ever built a decent pair of thighs without becoming intimately acquainted with the pain barrier, and then learning to smash through it set after set.

My off-season and precontest thigh workouts are quite similar. The only real difference between the two is the addition of a few extra sets of thigh work close to a show. And prior to a contest I generally increase my training pace. This faster workout pace inevitably necessitates a reduction in my exercise poundages. I have added the Weider Peak Contraction, and Slow, Continuous Tension Training Principles to my training and this more than makes up for the lighter workout poundages. Combining all of these precontest factors and techniques brings out the utmost in thigh shape, cuts, and symmetry.

Here are two examples of my thigh workouts:

Off-Season

1. Leg Press (45-degree angle): 6–8 × 8–10 (6–8 sets of 8–10 repetitions).
2. Squat: 4–5 × 8–10.
3. Leg Extension: 5–6 × 8–10.
4. Lying Leg Curl: 7–8 × 8–10.

Precontest

1. Leg Press (45-degree angle): 6–8 × 10–15 (6–8 sets of 10–15 repetitions).
2. Hack Squat: 5–6 × 10–15.
3. Squat: 5–6 × 10–15.
4. Leg Extension: 6–8 × 10–15.
5. Standing Leg Curl: 4–5 × 10–15.
6. Lying Leg Curl: 4–5 × 10–15.

I don't do supersets prior to a competition, but I do use the Weider Quality Training Principle, meaning I gradually reduce the rest intervals I take between sets. You'll notice that I use somewhat higher reps prior to a competition. I usually do these reps with the same poundage for every set of a particular exercise. By contrast, I usually pyramid my weights and reps in the off-season, adding 10–30 pounds to the bar or machine for each succeeding set of each exercise.

When a competition is approaching, I consider

it essential to practice poses for every part of my body—and especially for my thighs. I do this by flexing my thighs very hard for 10–15 seconds. This technique is called the Weider Iso-Tension Contraction Training Principle and Joe Weider taught it to me a few months ago.

If you have ever had any trouble bringing out the definition in your quadriceps, give Iso-Tension a try. It's done more for ripping up my thighs than any other technique I've ever tried. In fact, I just could never adequately isolate and display my sartorius muscles before I began using Iso-Tension Contraction. Now they snap out in bold relief during my posing routine!

Obviously, my Olympian-level thigh-training program would be totally inappropriate for beginning and intermediate bodybuilders. But if you have trained consistently for 1–2 years, you should be able to handle these workouts without overtraining.

Beginners can benefit from a thigh workout like this one for the first 1–3 months of bodybuilding training:

1. Squat: 1 × 15; 1 × 12; 1 × 10; 1 × 8.
2. Leg Extension: 3 × 10–12.
3. Leg Curl: 4–5 × 10–12.

When you do Squats, increase the resistance by 10–15 pounds after completing each set. This is the pyramidding (increasing resistance while decreasing reps) I mentioned earlier.

I seldom wear a lifting belt while squatting, but if you feel more secure when you wear one, go ahead. And if you are unsteady while squatting flat-footed, you can rest your heels on a 2″ × 4″ board to improve your equilibrium. Whether you use the board or not, your toes should be pointed outward at approximately 45-degree angles on each side and your heels should be no more than 12–14 inches apart as you do your Squats. Squatting with an excessively wide foot placement works the inner parts of your thighs too much.

Notice in this beginners' workout that I stress a greater-than-normal number of sets of Leg Curls. In my opinion, less than 5% of all bodybuilders have good thigh biceps development. So the beginner should start working on this area early in his or her career to ensure good development. Leg Curls are great for building thigh biceps. You can do this exercise either lying facedown on a leg machine, or standing erect and curling one leg at a time on one of the special Leg Curl machines, like the ones they have at Gold's and World Gym in California.

Surprisingly, you can also work your thigh biceps fairly hard when you do your back routine. I've found that Stiff-Leg Deadlifts provide equal stress to the thigh biceps muscles and erector spinae. You can easily prove this to yourself by not doing Deadlifts for 2–3 weeks and then doing 3–4 sets of Stiff-Leg Deadlifts (10–15 reps per set). To get a full range of motion you should do this exercise while standing on a flat exercise bench. The backs of your legs will be unbelievably sore the next day—a sure indication that Stiff-Leg Deadlifts really stress the thigh biceps.

When you move up to the intermediate training level, I suggest that you use this routine for 4–6 weeks:

1. Leg Extension: 4–5 × 10–12 (4–5 sets of 10–12 reps).
2. Leg Press (45-degree angle): 1 × 15; 1 × 12; 1 × 10; 1 × 8; 1 × 6; 1 × 15.
3. Squat: 4–6 × 8–10.
4. Leg Curl: 6–8 × 10–12.

This will seem like a man-killing (or woman-killing) thigh routine, but you must train this hard if you hope to develop championship thighs.

A Leg Press machine with a 45-degree angle is great for bringing out the sweep of muscle on the outer edges of your thighs. And it's also good for adding muscular bulk just above your knees. I've actually come to prefer this movement to Squats, and once you give it a try I think you'll come to the same conclusion.

Of course, many readers will not have this particular Leg Press machine available. An alternative is to use either the vertical-style Leg Press machine or the Universal Gym horizontal-style machine. Both are good pieces of equipment, but they will not build the thighs as effectively as the 45-degree Leg Press machine.

When you do Leg Presses you should pyramid your weights and then finish off with a final 15-rep pump set. And since you'll be using extremely heavy weights for this movement, it is a good idea to warm up your knees and quads with a few sets of Leg Extensions before starting your Leg Press routine.

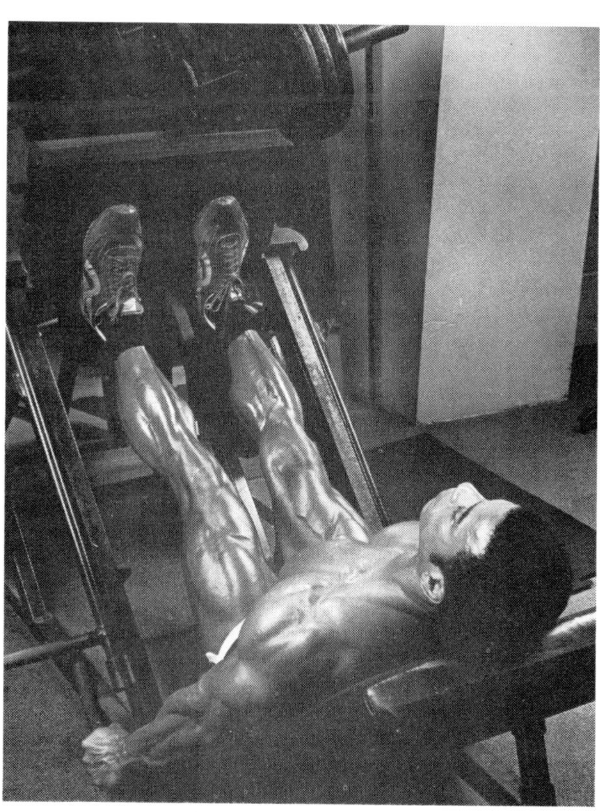

You should be very conscious of using a complete range of movement on all exercises, and particularly on Squats. You should squat to the lowest position you can comfortably reach. Ideally your calves should touch your hamstring muscles at the bottom position.

You can also use a "non-lock" technique when doing Squats and Leg Presses. This means you finish the movement when you're still a few inches away from a straight-leg position. This keeps continuous tension on your quadriceps, because a straight-leg position is actually a resting point for the thigh muscles. Used in this manner, the Weider Continuous Tension Training Principle is extremely effective in developing the inner thigh muscles just above the knees.

You can finish your intermediate-level routine with Leg Curls. I recommend stretching your thigh biceps muscles between sets of Leg Curls. You can do this by standing erect, keeping your knees locked, and then slowly bending forward. Bend until you feel a slightly painful sensation in your hamstrings, hold that position for 10–15 seconds, and then relax the stretch. If you consistently stretch your hamstrings between sets of Leg Curls, I'm confident you will accelerate your thigh biceps' growth rate by as much as 25%–30%.

At the beginning level of bodybuilding training, I recommend three workouts per week, e.g., Mondays, Wednesdays, and Fridays. You will be training your entire body on these days, including your thighs. But once you get to the intermediate level, you will probably be using a split routine, working half the body one day, the other half the next.

When you are using a split routine I suggest training your chest, shoulders, and arms on Mondays and Thursdays, your back and thighs on Tuesdays and Fridays. You can work your calves and abdominals on all four training days. A split like this will allow your body to recuperate more fully from each workout and hence grow at a faster rate. Unless you have a contest coming up, you should not train on a six-day split routine. Four–five weeks before competing you can start doing a six-day split to sharpen up for your show.

After at least a year of hard thigh training, you can start doing a workout similar to the one I use in the off-season. However, I suggest you do this routine only twice per week, rather than three times a week as I do. Of course, it will take a great deal of pain, sweat, and hard work to bring your thighs up to Olympian standard. But if you train them hard and consistently, you will be well on the way to winning some big titles.